Teaching Navigation

Practical ideas for outdoor tutors

by Nigel Williams

on behalf of the
National Navigation Award Scheme

NNAS
a step in the right direction

HARVEY

Published and distributed by:

HARVEY, 12–22 Main Street, Doune, Perthshire FK16 6BJ
Tel: 01786 841202
email: sales@harveymaps.co.uk

Published 2018

ISBN 9781851376087
© 2018 National Navigation Award Scheme

Supported by:

National Navigation Award Scheme
Office 17
Stirling Enterprise Park,
Stirling FK7 7RP
Tel: 01786 451307
Fax: 01786 445703
Email: info@nnas.org.uk
www.nnas.org.uk

About the Author

Nigel Williams
Nigel was the Head of Training at Glenmore Lodge, Scotland's National Mountain Training Centre, for 20 years and has a range of outdoor qualifications in mountaineering, orienteering and Nordic skiing. After a 16-year period in the military, much of it spent on expeditions and adventure training, he worked for Fife Council in outdoor education before joining the National Mountain Training Centre.

Nigel has been teaching navigation for more than 40 years both in the military and working in outdoor education. Working on Mountain Training courses, as an orienteering coach and a NNAS tutor has provided a significant insight into the different approaches and relevance of the navigation teaching methodologies in use in the UK.

Acknowledgements
Firstly to Tom Renfrew and Terry O'Brien who inspired me with a whole new approach to teaching the subject on an orienteering instructors course in 1994. Dan Riley, British Orienteering Services Officer and Pat Mee author of the original Outdoor Navigation Handbook for tutors. James Woodhouse, Margaret Porter and members of the NNAS Board for their support in the project. The many staff and students who have come through Glenmore Lodge and offered ideas and encouragement over the years. Sue Harvey and her team for the support, in particular Chris Beacock for his patience, design and production.

Contents

Teaching Navigation

Introduction

The ideas in this manual are a foundation for introducing the basic concepts of navigation. Books on teaching orienteering and the National Navigation Award Scheme (NNAS) Handbook for Tutors will offer further ideas. The approach taken forms a systematic, dynamic method for teaching people to navigate for outdoor recreation, as opposed to static map reading which has been the basis of teaching the subject for many decades.

There are many good books on mountain navigation but outside of the sport of orienteering there is virtually nothing on how to teach the subject in a structured and relevant manner. Those who teach navigation for recreation are generally not attracted to a book cover with pictures of lycra-clad orienteers running through a forest; however orienteers are probably the best on-foot navigators in the world. The question is: how did they get so good at navigating, especially when you consider that they use maps with just north lines, and compasses with no numbers and dials that don't turn?

Involving numeracy when teaching the basics of navigation can be a negative experience for some students. With the exception of pacing and distance measurement, all the skills of on-the-move navigation, including compass work, can be taught without the need for numbers, which are mostly introduced for the purposes of communicating or sharing a place or direction.

Being able to work out a grid reference has never helped anyone on the move to navigate a route. Whilst a route card is useful as a planning tool, once disorientated or off the prescribed route, it is not going to help recover the situation; only navigation skills will do that.

Today young people expect quick success and rewards for their efforts. Orienteering-scale maps offer a great deal more navigational decisions to be made in a short space of time, and in a less intimidating environment compared with being out on the hill. They make it easier for the tutor and the student to set targets, get feedback, see results, gain confidence and have fun outdoors in a relatively non-threatening environment where almost every obvious feature that is visible on the ground is on the map.

The orienteering map is to teaching navigation what the indoor climbing wall was to teaching rock climbing 30 years ago. These maps are cheap and now much more available all over the UK. Many urban parks have orienteering maps which are free to download. Most schools now have an orienteering map of their grounds, and sometimes orienteering clubs also have maps available online. It is now much easier to ensure each individual has a map (which can be laminated to prolong its life). However it should be remembered that having a map does not give a right of access.

Being able to navigate with a map is a life skill. If we can reduce barriers through the teaching process, we might hopefully reduce a barrier to people taking outdoor exercise and exploring beyond the front door or car.

How navigation is taught within the education system would appear to be a matter of who introduces the young people to the subject first. The geography teacher has to teach map reading as a part of the examination process, and starts with symbols, scales and grid references- a largely static classroom-based approach. The PE or extra curricular activities teacher might start with active learning, largely outdoors, with an orienteering map. There appears to be no course within education specifically aimed at teaching the subject or marrying up the diverse range of approaches.

Benchmarking of competence against a system of progressions for both tutors and students could provide a more universal approach across the outdoor sector in its widest form. It could enhance Accredited Prior Learning (APL), knowledge transfer and pathways between outdoor activities.

This manual aims to provide a simple set of progressions and ideas for teaching the techniques of on-the-move recreational navigation.

Preparing to move off

History

Much of traditional navigation teaching has been geared around the past needs of the military and is over-complicated for recreational needs. Britain has the best mapping in the world but still teaches the subject based on an 80 year-old methodology which stems from the introduction of grid lines in 1936 by the Ordnance Survey (OS) which at that time was a part of the military. It is a static map reading process based on plotting trenches, observation posts, artillery etc, and then communicating that information as a grid reference to other units. For greater precision military compasses use mils – 6,400 to a circle, instead of 360 degrees. (An angle of 1 mil measures one metre at a distance of a kilometre; the circumference of a circle one kilometre out from the centre measures 6400 metres.) That level of accuracy explains why magnetic variation is considered important, especially for aiming artillery. Accuracy was vital and an error could have fatal consequences for your own side.

The military used prismatic sighting compasses without a base plate. Bearings were taken off the map with a protractor and then transferred to the compass. The baseplate compass we use today was invented in 1928, but would not have been commonly available until some time later. (Compared with a prismatic compass with mils, it is less accurate). The base plate has the protractor built in which enables us to take a bearing off the map, aim and follow it with a single device.

The use of maps for outdoor recreation was not in their thinking back then and the teaching methodology has struggled to evolve in line with the popularity of outdoor activities and the development of compasses and larger-scale, more detailed maps.

Youth organisations such as Scouts date back to 1908, the three Service Cadet Forces were formally recognised in the 1940s, DofE started in 1956, Ten Tors on Dartmoor originated in 1959, Mountain Training in 1964, all basing navigation teaching on the military system passed on from trainer to trainer. There was no alternative methodology available at the time these organisations came into being.

The easily available 1:50,000 scale OS map (replacing the old 1-inch-to-the-mile map) led tutors to teach indoors for several reasons. The maps were expensive so there were not enough for one per student. Often they were not of the immediate local area, so almost any navigation technique practised on the ground required travelling to a mapped area. It was easier to remain in the classroom sharing maps, working out grid references, bearings, magnetic variation and theoretical resections to help determine one's location.

Orienteering arrived in the UK in the early 1960s but it was a further decade before it became well established with a simple and coherent teaching methodology which started to produce world-class navigators. However, the outdoor recreation fraternity seemed to view it as a minority sport. The maps were few and far between and primitive by today's standards. The dress code at the time, akin to pyjamas, probably didn't help either. Today British Orienteering offers a range of courses for teachers and coaches and the sport is developing exciting new formats such as sprint orienteering for the urban environment, and mountain bike orienteering, to attract a wider range of outdoor enthusiasts.

The National Navigation Award Scheme (NNAS) was established in 1994 by Peter Palmer who was a teacher, a high level orienteer and coach. He recognised that navigation skills are universal to outdoor activities and the teaching of the subject should reflect the user needs and be an active learning process.

The National Navigation Award Scheme has now come of age with a formal tutor training programme. The Bronze NNAS award is recognised on the Scottish Credits and Qualifications Framework (SCQF) which in turn is attracting the youth organisations to the scheme and its teaching methodology.

Mountain bike orienteering is a relatively new format which attracts a wider range of outdoor enthusiasts

Building confidence and having fun

Someone once said navigation is probably 25% map reading, 25% compass work and 50% confidence in the other two. After many years of teaching navigation, I fully concur with that summary.

The most important principle in teaching navigation should be to build confidence through progressions of practical and interesting exercises at every stage. Part of the adventure is eventually having an opportunity to make decisions independent of the tutor.

British Orienteering believes that a first experience of orienteering should:

- Be fun, exciting and adventurous
- Be well presented, supportive and easy to understand
- Be challenging, with regular feedback and a chance to experience success
- Be engaging, safe and of a suitable length for the individual's needs
- Ensure each participant has a map of their own and learns something about navigation.

This should be the aspiration for anyone teaching navigation. As the ultimate aim of this book is to give people confidence in using regular OS or Harvey mapping for recreation in the outdoors, 'using an appropriate environment' could be added to the list for our purposes.

Tools of progression

There are a number of variables that can be juggled to help the learning process and also make coaching the subject fun for the tutor.

A step system and lesson plans
A clear sequence of skills development is well understood in orienteering and the National Navigation Award Scheme (NNAS). They both use a table of progressive steps. Whilst some orienteering language diverges from the language of the hill-goer, the principle of steady building block progressions, in an appropriate environment for learning, is very important to all.

The progressions outlined here should be seen as a guide. Occasionally a situation arises providing a good teaching opportunity out-of-sequence. If working with an older group who have had prior tuition, some subjects may be approached differently, or in a different order. However, a good structure

and knowledge of the teaching processes will help manage these opportunities effectively.

A range of coaching methodologies can be used throughout the progressions and the different games and exercises provide a flexible approach towards reaching student autonomy. Once tutors are familiar with these, and how long they might take, it will be possible to design a structured programme and brief lesson plans which will help manage resources, from venues to mapping and minibuses.

Stepped approach to teaching navigation
The stepped approach table (see p.4) for teaching and learning navigation has been adapted from other models but using the language of the hillwalker. Ideally each step should be completed, including feedback that the students have grasped the concepts and skills, prior to moving on. These notes provide ideas for coaching each step and evaluating the students' understanding of the techniques and concepts.

There is a mass of games and exercises at the early stages of learning to navigate, but even the most complex skills can be broken down and coached with some short fun exercises on a large-scale map before putting them into context on a smaller scale map.

For example:
Taking a bearing cross-country is a sophisticated multi-tasking process. Consider all the elements that are involved and how they could be taught individually using progressions of mapping and different environments.

1. Taking a bearing from the map
2. Measuring a distance on the map
3. Measuring distance on the ground
4. Following and staying accurately on a bearing on the ground
5. Ticking off features, thumbing and reading the ground and map (see p.7)
6. Identifying and using catching features if the target is missed. That then leads on to the ability either to retrace a route or use a relocation strategy.

Consider further progressions and exercises to help combine the individual skills and develop underpinning knowledge and practice.

What becomes apparent is that the different step

A stepped approach to teaching navigation for outdoor recreation

LEVEL 1 **The basics**	• Introduce the concepts of maps: symbols, scale, cardinal points and map setting. Indoors and centre/school grounds. • Outdoor map setting exercises, map walks extending the environment, interpreting the key and map setting. • Thumbing – keeping track of progress along simple line features. • Introduce the compass needle for map setting only. • Basic distance judgement, measuring distances on the map and ground. Introduce pacing and timing on the flat. All above using a large-scale map. • Introduce the 1:25,000 maps. Local map walk on tracks, actively learning and bringing the above skills together. • Grid references. **Map setting is the most fundamental concept of navigation.**
LEVEL 2 **Developing skills**	• Starting relocation skills: resetting the map with and without the compass needle and processing information to help locate a position. • Identifying and using simple physical catching features. • Introduction of contours for major ground shapes. Feeling the ground shape underfoot. • Quick bearings along line features used for confirmation of route at junctions and simple relocation strategies. All the above using a large-scale map. • Introduce 1:40,000 or 1:50,000 scale maps. Map walk along tracks to familiarise the scale and symbols. **Plan and travel along a route which follows line features. Estimating the distance and time required.**
LEVEL 3 **Compass skills** **Route planning** **Developing strategies**	• Introduce quick bearings for short distances across country 50–100m. • Route planning strategies: aiming off, catching features, attack points, boxing or dog legs etc. • Introduce fine bearings using the compass off the map. • Recognising detailed contour features: knolls and re-entrants etc. • Recognising where contours create linear features and the relationship they have with the direction of travel; feeling the contours. • Using a variety of techniques to achieve navigation legs across open ground. • Relocation strategies, using line features and slope aspect. A system 'Move to prove' or 'Travel to unravel'. • All the above can be taught using a large-scale map before applying to smaller scale walking maps. **Independent accurate navigation on and off line features using basic strategies in hill and moorland terrain.**
LEVEL 4 **Complex hill navigation**	• Summer navigating using only landform features on 1:25,000 - 1:50,000 maps • Develop confidence and strategies for independent navigation in poor visibility or darkness. • Introduce other devices – altimeters and GPS – and use them in conjunction with other navigation tools. **Selecting the right mix of skills for economic and efficient navigation including relocation in the UK mountains in non-winter conditions.**
LEVEL 5 **Full winter navigation**	• Operating under full winter conditions including whiteout, using contours only and a mix of strategies in order to manage winter hazards and maintain a good level of accuracy with map and compass.

This table provides progressions through the skills as well as map scale and environment to help maximise learning time and skills development. **Building confidence at each level before moving to the next is key.**

levels correspond well to outdoor qualifications. Level 2 for instance, **"plan and travel along a route which follows line features and estimating the distance and time required"**, is the requirement of Mountain Training's Lowland Leader Award, Bronze DofE, NNAS Bronze, British Cycling Mountain Bike Leader level 2 (with the addition of using a trip computer) and British Canoeing Moderate Water Leadership awards. Level 3 would be Hill and Moorland Leader and Level 4, Mountain Leader (summer) upwards with Level 5 being Winter, Mountain Leader and Mountain Instructors Certificate.

Map scale

There can be confusion as to which is a large or small scale map. Large scales in this context are usually 1:1,000, 1:5,000, 1:10,000 or 1:15,000 orienteering-style maps with lots of information and detail, excellent for learning the basics of all navigation skills. These maps are generally made of school grounds, parks and forests. They are more conducive to learning and practice than smaller scale maps. It surely makes sense to start with a large-scale map which has virtually everything marked that a beginner sees and can relate to around them before moving onto smaller scales. Large-scale maps enable better supervision in the early stages of teaching as they enable close tutor support, more repetition and therefore more feedback and improved learning opportunities to build confidence.

Smaller scale maps in this context are 1:40,000, and 1:50,000 and these, together with 1:25,000 are the scale of maps that walkers generally use. They are good for rural and hill areas, as they cover a large area for a day's walk, but have less detailed information and therefore require more interpretation and confidence.

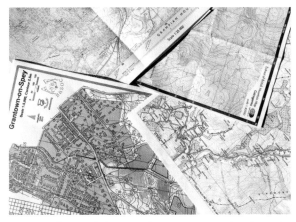

A range of maps helps provide progressions of scale and remoteness

Environment and remoteness

It is best to start teaching navigation using a large-scale map in familiar nearby terrain to stop external factors getting in the way of the leaarning process. Working with a 1:25,000 scale would seem appropriate before moving to 1:40,000 or 1:50,000 scales which progressively have less information on them. Environmental progressions can start in the classroom and move on to the gym, the grounds, the local forest and eventually the hills. At each stage the map scale and environment will change. Inclement weather on a hillside with a 1:50,000 map may leave a novice feeling outside their comfort zone and is unlikely to provide a good learning outcome.

If the participants have a sound foundation of the skills, then remoteness and weather will have a much reduced impact on learning, and may even present an exciting challenge. In addition, once using 1:25,000 or 1:50,000 map scales, the distances to be travelled (both with transport to a venue as well as on foot) to practice navigation are likely to be greater. In other words smaller scale maps are generally better for practice and applying skills. For learning new skills choose a large scale map.

Teaching groups

At the outset it helps to have everyone working together in a small, contained and familiar environment where they can have some fun and the tutor is close at hand for support and feedback. A variety of well recognised teaching practices can be used involving peer feedback, student-led exercises and so on. Sending students out on their own when they are not ready for it can have a significant impact on their confidence and further engagement with the subject. An easy group management progression to consider as skills and trust develop between the tutor and pupils is:

On site – in sight

On site – out of sight

Off site – in sight

Off site – out of sight

It is a progression of letting go: a progressive approach to giving participants independence from their teacher/instructor. When making decisions which, one way or another, will have a consequence, steady progressions help that consequence to be positive.

Timing

How much time or how many sessions the coach has to teach the subject will influence which progressions, maps and environments will be used. The timing of introducing new skills, moving to more remote environments and on to map scales with less information, can be critical to success or disappointment. It will also depend on the group and their existing navigation knowledge and outdoor experience. Tutors ponder over these decisions at length when reviewing their sessions.

Summary

Teaching navigation should be structured but enjoyable. It is also a responsibility, as navigation can be a skill for life. We rarely get it right every time for every student. Practice helps and also leads to tutor confidence. It is important to plan and review the processes, successes and challenges and try things differently next time around. Students enjoy a variety of learning and so do coaches. Adapt and improvise and rarely will you run a session where you do not learn or tweak something for next time.

It is important for tutors to practise their own navigation skills as this helps to learn new ideas and to experiment with them. There are a range of other opportunities available to develop navigation coaching, from orienteering to NNAS and Mountain Training awards.

The structure of the book

The book is separated into five skills sections, followed by several other supporting sections. The first two sections lead through a series of progressions largely based around the map and following linear or handrail features. Section 3 develops compass skills, although the compass is introduced in the first sections. 4 and 5 continue with progressions but are topic-based. Once the navigator has the map and compass skills, these topics are more around strategies and putting the skills into context. Parts of them will be drip fed through the earlier sections at appropriate opportunities or through student curiosity and questions.

Navigation can be a skill for life

Section 1: The Basics of Navigation

Understanding and interpreting the map key, or legend

Map setting and ground interpretation are the core skills; everything else is an aid to effective navigation. When following a linear feature (like a path) with the map orientated, the only requirements are knowledge of the map symbols and contours, with a sense of the scale; there is no need for a compass, knowledge of navigation strategies or relocation techniques.

Learning to read a map and relate it to the ground should be an active process where the learner discovers the map symbols for themselves. Ideally use a short 'map walk' on a large-scale map in an area that would not feel remote to the participants. If it is an enclosed area it might be possible safely to send pupils out in pairs for 15 minutes with a map but no key and see who can identify the most symbols. Large-scale maps have plenty of detail for the novice to see and be inquisitive about. Whilst some symbols on these maps may vary, there are in fact plenty of similarities. Passively memorising 1:50,000 scale map symbols in a classroom without seeing the feature on the ground does not inspire as a starting point for learning to navigate.

Using a large-scale map while walking along a path or track also helps with map setting. Students tend to do this automatically, and quickly make sense of the information around them. The quick feedback provided by 1:5,000 or 1:10,000 orienteering scales is a real confidence builder from the start.

An ice-breaker session - map jigsaws
Briefly introduce navigation and the aims of the session. Use four or five orienteering maps (can be downloaded and don't need to be local) with a good variety of colours, features and a key on them. These are best laminated and cut into pieces of different shapes and sizes (an A4 map sheet would be in about eight pieces). Randomly distribute the pieces among the class. It is a group task to re-assemble the maps. They will do this easily by recognition of symbols and shapes, the start of map reading skills. It starts to give them confidence with a map. Congratulate them on being able to read it!

Using an orienteering map is helpful if that is the type of map to be used for subsequent map walks, so ask a few questions about what different colours and symbols represent. A similar exercise could be done with smaller-scale OS or Harvey maps prior to

starting to navigate with them. It stimulates thought around the symbols.

A quick clarification of the cardinal points N, S, E, W, may be helpful. Avoid getting into degrees or the Earth's magnetism etc; it is the relationship between the points which is useful.

Figure 1.1 Classroom ice-breaker exercise leading into familiarisation with the orienteering map scale and symbols

Map setting, thumbing, simple symbols, scale
For a group of around 6 to 20 complete beginners, start in the classroom, with a number of desks laid out and a sheet or two of A4 paper and a writing implement on each one.

A map is a two-dimensional plan of three dimensional objects. To illustrate this with youngsters consider starting with an empty desk or a mat on the floor. This can be drawn first from the bird's-eye view – just a square/oblong. Then place a few objects on it, as in Figure 1.2 below. Look at these from above and draw them (stand on a chair if necessary). The mug lying down appears as an oblong shape to the mapper yet the upright mug is a circle. The learners

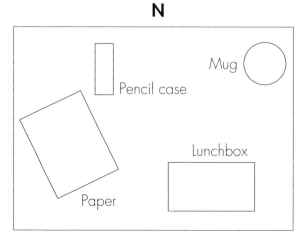

Figure 1.2 Tabletop diagram

are creating a two dimensional plan, a map, and understanding relative positions of things. Put an N marker for north on the table/floor. They should mark that on their plan. Next ask them to rotate their map so it is not set to the table and point out the discrepancies and the importance of setting. Then with it correctly set, try walking around the model and matching their map to it on each side. Although it makes no difference in the classroom, if north is always indicated close to reality it provides continuity in the student's mind, and may reduce the possibility of confusion later on with a map of the grounds.

Classroom mapmaking and setting

With an older group this may be a more appropriate starting point. Starting with a blank sheet of paper ask them to depict the room as they would see it if they could fly over it if there was no roof and nothing in it i.e. the four walls only. Each person usually draws a different size. (With an oblong room there is no need to draw anything, as an A4 sheet is the same shape.) To illustrate scale, compare two different sized diagrams, and ask which is correct. They both are of course. It is just a matter of scale. One map might represent a wall three thumbnails wide. If the room measured 300 thumbnails wide on the floor then one thumbnail on the map represents 100 on the ground i.e. 1:100 scale. A bigger map might measure 10 thumbnails wide representing a 1:30 scale. If the classroom is an awkward shape it may be easier to pre-draw and photocopy the outline.

Ensure everyone has drawn the room as big as they can on their sheet. It is often helpful and fun to join in, and a tutor map provides an example to show at each stage of the drawing. Place a large letter N on one wall of the room (preferably a wall that is somewhere near north) and ask them to identify the relevant wall on their map, and add a big N and scribble along that side. (The scribble is so that you can see from a distance later in the session that they have their maps set.) It may also help to give the map a name and put that on the north end (similar to a real map). Ask them to match the orientation of the map to the room.

Next… Draw in desks and any obvious flat surfaces which the group might have to negotiate their way around later on, though not each chair. Mark a triangle for where they are sitting, and ensure all the maps are basically the same. (If you do not know the group, it is a good way of getting to know them by writing in each individual's name against where they are sitting). Now get them to turn their maps, disori-

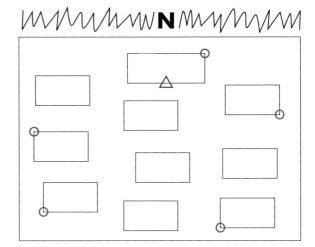

Figure 1.3 Classroom diagram

entating them and recognise the map-to-ground discrepancies.

Next… Ask the group to stand up and navigate around their desk, keeping the map set but walking normally, not backwards or sideways. Keeping the map set requires the navigator to move their body around the map keeping the north scribbled end of the map orientated towards the N on the wall. It feels as though they are turning the map in their fingers but in reality they are moving around it.

Next… Have prepared about five little markers (sticky notes, about 3cm square, see p.42 for commercial suppliers). On each one is a small letter. Go around the room placing them at various points. Use common map language, for instance where the walls meet in a corner you might call it a 'fence junction'. You may have to explain a junction. If there is a flip chart or a TV on a tall stand you might call it a 'knoll' and explain a knoll. If a desk is a wood you might put a marker on a corner. Ask: which corner is it? South west etc. As you place the markers around the room the students should put a small circle on their map where the marker is. Each person should now have created something like the classroom diagram shown in Figure 1.3.

Next… Using their maps, the class navigate around the room and write down the letter that is on each of the markers next to the circle on the map. There are a couple of rules to give them:

• You must thumb your map and read your way around the furniture, visiting the markers in any order. Thumbing is the technique of keeping one's thumb or possibly a finger, on the map and using it to follow the route you are travelling along. It enables the navigator to keep track of their progress and locate their position on the map at a glance. Do not just look across the room and head to the next marker without using the map.

• You must always have your map set. (The scribbled north end of their map will enable the tutor to verify this from a distance).

Next… Once back at their desk ask them to draw in a random route from their triangle linking all the circles. An example is shown in Figure 1.4 below.

• It must link up all the markers and lead back to their triangle.

• Number each marker as they come to it: 1, 2, 3 etc.

• Mark arrows along their line route to show the direction of travel.

• The route should go around any of the pieces of furniture they have drawn.

• Lastly encourage them to be imaginative in their route.

You complete your own map as well.

(A dotted line could go under tables and a solid line could go over the tops of tables but do consider safety issues, the furniture, class control, time available etc, as this can become chaotic).

This has even been done in the dark with headtorches on a winter's evening!

Now comes the crunch for the unsuspecting class. Leave their maps where they are and change places with someone else. Using another person's map,

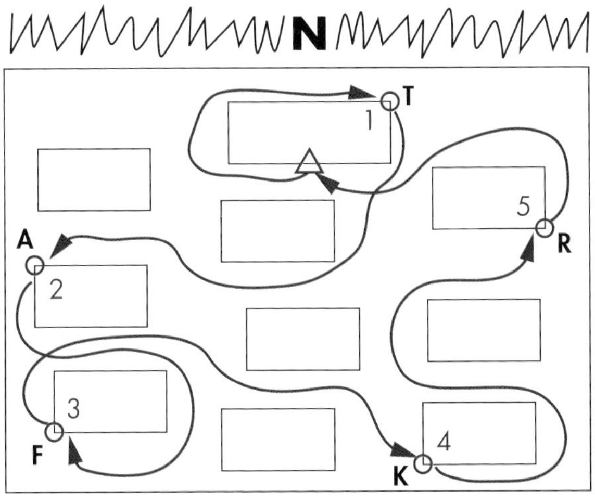

follow the same rules as before. Follow the route on the map to check that their colleague has recorded the correct letter at each location. If the tutor has made a map, they can join in too, whilst checking that the group are thumbing their way around with their maps set, and finally returning to the start point.

Next… Move the class around onto another map. This time ask them to pick up the map, lock their elbows into their sides and imagine their hands are super-glued to the map so they cannot turn it. Walking forwards, they now try to follow the marked route without being able to keep the map set. Alternatively, before leaving the last map, have them rotate it 180° and leaving it on the table. The group now change places, picking up a new map and trying to navigate their route, keeping it set 180° out. This will prove extremely difficult and it is best to stop the session almost immediately because the point is made how hard it is to navigate without the map being set. Essentially they feel lost in the classroom!

End the session by collecting in the bits and pieces. Finally, we always "leave the environment as we found it", so collect all the markers and the 'N' off the wall.

A whole range of knowledge has now been covered: from map making and symbols, to scale, thumbing, map orientation and map language, and they have been able to read and understand someone else's map. The same principles can be confirmed with similar exercises in a gymnasium or hall, green mats could be forest, blue mats a loch, benches a track, a vaulting horse is a knoll etc, and there are many more games that can be played with starting points around the edge of the hall.

An additional exercise would be to work in pairs and memorise each other's routes, then follow them around the classroom without the map. This works best in the gym.

To evaluate whether the group has understood the concept of map setting and thumbing before you move onto the next stage, the following exercises will prove extremely effective and fun.

Figure 1.4 Classroom map with route joining all points from start triangle back to triangle, all points numbered and arrows showing direction of travel

Nine-cone exercises

Introduction

Map setting is the single most important skill that underpins all navigation. These simple exercises can follow classroom setting exercises or be a starting point for novices. A map walk with an orienteering map immediately following these exercises will bring it all into context.

Using two colours of cards (say ten yellow and ten blue) mark up a route on each yellow card and then duplicate the set on the blue cards. (See page 42 for a source of ready-made card sets for these exercises). Number the pairs of cards on the back for ease of sorting and finally laminate them all.

A set of ten pairs can be made progressively more complex. There is a huge number of routes that can be designed: six to nine legs will provide a range of difficulty, and start and finish points should always be on corners. Lines crossing may create confusion, so make the route clear by breaking the crossover line and putting in some direction arrows. A triangle is the start and double circle the finish. See Figure 1.5.

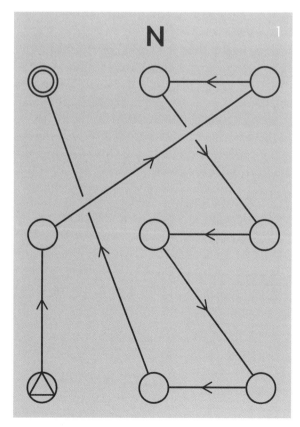

Figure 1.5 Nine point map card

Set-up

The circles on the cards represent nine markers which can be laid out using chalk on tarmac or a gym floor, or on a smooth area of grass with anything you have ten of. Plastic sports marker cones are good.

For continuity it may be helpful to lay out the grid of cones aligned roughly to north on the ground. Place them in an oblong pattern approximately 12 steps long, six steps wide; too big an area and people have too much time to think, too small and they are likely to collide.

Clearly identify north on the ground by marking a large N on a 10th cone. Place that cone at the north end to represent the N on the cards.

Explanation

Put the group into pairs. Each pair should have two cards with the same design but of different colours. Explain the set-up standing at the south end of the cones. It seems more logical for the group to look at the layout from that perspective, and to set the map (the card, in this case) with the N on the card aligned to the pattern on the ground.

With very young people it may help to stand at the edge of the cone grid with card in hand correctly set. Indicate a particular cone. Get them to point out that cone on their map (card). Then do the same from map to ground. With youngsters, a variety of colours of cones can help.

A triangle shows the start. Finish at the double circle. As they move they can follow the route with a thumb on the map. 'Thumbing' the map helps keep track of where they are.

Give a quick demonstration using one of the group as a static partner who checks your route from the triangle start point. This illustrates that only one of the pair goes around the route while the other one watches and checks their partner is following the route correctly. Jog around and keep the map constantly set as you go, holding the map in both hands so your body is 'going around the map' at each turn.

Before the group sets off, get them to hold the map in front of them with both hands and move 360 degrees around their map. Although it feels like they are turning the map in their hands, in fact their body is going around it and the map stays in the same relationship to the ground.

Figure 1.6 Map setting around the cones

Safety

It is important to warn the group to watch where they are going, as once people start racing around they may collide. Also warn of slipping on wet grass; check they have suitable footwear.

Exercise 1

Set them off by calling for all of one colour of card to go first. Afterwards those with the other colour have a go.

After each person has had a go, swap pairs of cards, repeat the exercise and start to get them jogging so the whole setting and thumbing process has to be really slick.

Working with an unset map

To illustrate the importance of map setting, ask the group to follow the route on a new pair of cards but without turning the map. Tell them to hold the card with elbows into their sides, and imagining their hands are super-glued to the card. They cannot rotate the card once they set off nor are they allowed to run sideways or backwards, although some will. Before starting them off, just ask how they would normally walk along a path. (Forwards you hope). Most are quickly disorientated and it proves the

point about map setting. Finish off the exercise with a couple more practices at setting the map to leave them with the right impression.

This fun exercise links the concept of map setting with a practical and memorable exercise. With the unset map people are often seen doing two things: trying to commit the route to memory – using 'map memory' (especially the second person), and trying to relocate at the markers by turning their body to temporarily set the map to work out the next leg – using 'relocation skills'. Identifying these actions provides a great link into the next exercises. Give positive feedback to the group that they were doing the right things and introduce the map memory and relocation exercises.

Exercise 2 – Map memory

Picking up on the non-setting exercise above, give one card to each pair. They go to the indicated start point. The first person has 30 seconds to memorise the card, then hands it to their partner and runs the route from memory. The partner watches to check the route is correct. Remember to swap cards around the group so the second person does not have an advantage.

Exercise 3 – Relocation skills

This exercise introduces the idea of relocation skills through map setting. The group stands outside the area of the markers. The tutor stands within the area holding all the cards. Look at the first card, select a point about half-way around the route and stand at it. Call forward the first volunteer and give them the card which is disorientated and turned over. They then have to set it, locate where they are and follow the route to the end. Continue with the next card in hand often running between cones to give a different starting point for each person.

Summary

The simplicity of the nine point exercises is that they are memorable and make it easy to manage and support the learner. It brings out a number of basic skills which you can refer back to once a real map is in hand. One can usually find ten (nine, plus a north marker) of something: rucsacs, jackets, rocks etc. This set of cards is easily carried and the exercises can be done almost anywhere there is room.

There are a number of similar exercises. Orienteers use up to 16 or even 25 markers in a symmetrical pattern. However, running around a large number of points may create additional confusion, needs more resources and takes longer to set up.

Further notes and exercises

Map walk

Ideally, immediately after the card setting exercises above, hand each student a large-scale map of the area they are in. The map should be either a home-made map of a local area, a street map or an orienteering map. Avoid using a small-scale map. (With an adult group expecting to progress rapidly to other walking maps, pacing could be introduced at this point. However it is explained in Section 2).

Help the group to get an understanding of the key through simple questioning, then head out to walk a route on the map going around the building, grounds or park, with plenty of changes of direction to continue with the map setting theme. Follow line features (tracks and paths), thumbing and maintaining the map set to north using the ground. It is very much a 'walk-and-talk' exercise, pointing out obvious features on the ground and on the map and how they match in shape, size, alignment etc. 45 minutes is long enough. Folding the map to the area they are working on is also helpful.

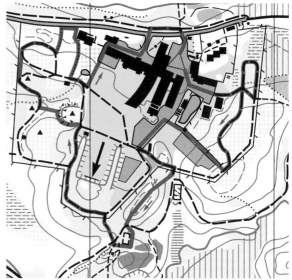

Figure 1.7 Map walk route shown in red, involving many changes of direction. Map © HARVEY

Ask what is coming next on the left or right side of the line feature. Put the map away and walk for a minute or so to an obvious feature, then ask where they are. Let one of them lead and ask questions of the others. The NNAS tutor handbook offers a few other similar exercises.

After a while the red end of the compass needle could be introduced for map setting. Prevent people turning the dial and lining up lines etc; it is unnecessary. Simply drop the compass on the map and turn the map with the compass on it until the red end of the needle points to the top of the map (north). The map and compass can be held in one hand with the compass on the side of the map and keeping the needle pointing to the top of the map.

Figure 1.8 Map and compass easily held in one hand

Make a map

This is best using a built-up area – a street map is an excellent starting point – lots of easy line features, a good scale and easy to set the map to the ground.

Check the local authority or community website as to whether there is a large-scale map of the local park. These are often free to download or available from the local tourist offices. Schools can go through the local authority for their grounds mapping. Educational establishments have access to digimaps which can be free to print at a 1:10,000 scale. Check the local orienteering club (www.britishorienteering.co.uk) who may have a map that would be useful. The website also has a list of over 500 Permanent Orienteering Courses (POCs) around the UK, most of which are free to download and print. **Please note: having a map may not give you a right of access.**

Maps can be made simply by pacing/measuring and using a compass. Digital mapping or even Google Earth may provide a starting point for creating your own map. All you need are photocopier, crayons and a laminator to preserve the map. Use the group to help create and colour in a map as a part of the learning process. **NOTE Most mapping is copyrighted and copying other than for personal use may require a licence.**

Star navigation exercises

These exercises run more easily with two members of staff. Use a map of a school grounds or a park, preferably open ground with reasonable visibility. Choose a central feature on the map to be the start and finish point. Identify a series of features around 50m away from the central point which are visible from the start point. Markers can be pre-placed, with a punch, or symbol to be recorded, as evidence of the students finding it. Students can go in pairs to start with, progressing to going solo if appropriate. They simply need to navigate back and forth between the start and marked points by setting the map.

Using this exercise will help reinforce map setting principles using a real map. It is very low-risk in terms of the consequences of making mistakes. The tutor can monitor how they are getting on and intervene if there is a problem.

Alternatively, good planning of this exercise may eliminate the need for the tutor to pre-place markers. Each individual/pair has a marker flag and the tutor marks a single location on each map. Each pair has a different map. From the central point individuals go out and place their marker at the assigned feature and return to the start. (The tutor ought to be able to see roughly where the marker should be placed and intervene if a student is heading wildly

off). The students then swap maps with their partner so another person can now go and recover the marker. The maps are swapped around between the pairs and the exercise is repeated.

After a few goes at that, the students place their marker and return. Next, the tutor marks a second point on each map and maps are swapped around. Individuals now go to point A where the marker was left, pick it up and take it to the second point B on their map then return to the centre where the tutor adds another point and maps are swapped and markers visited and moved. After a couple of goes at that with all the markers out, the students can navigate around all of them before returning to the centre (but leaving the markers in place, so that markers are not removed before someone has time to visit them). As confidence builds in the students and the tutor, the markers could be placed out of sight of the tutor and the distances expanded. This could even be expanded into a wooded area with a competent group.

Figure 1.9 A round map. Map © HARVEY

Round maps

Round maps present a bigger challenge to keep the map set and read the ground. Make one up from an existing map. Use a small plate as a template to cut out a circular map. Try to ensure there is no writing on the map at all, just a start triangle and a circle for each point, otherwise there is a tendency to set the map to read the writing.

Line courses

A further exercise might be to place some markers along a simple track route and ask the group to go along the track and individually mark on their maps where the markers are. This requires the individual to keep the map set, thumb the map and tick off all the features in order to know where they and the markers are. It may also be a good exercise after pacing has been taught and could allow for progression to more random placement of markers at featureless points along a track.

Map memory card games

A few sets of map memory cards are great for a 15-minute gap at the end of a lesson. Postcard-size is ideal, but it is useful to have two colours of card. In each set there should be six pairs (six of each colour). Use two identical maps of any scale (photocopying is easy). Cut out identical squares from each map approximately 3cm square. Stick one piece on each of the two coloured cards, creating a set of six pairs. On the same side under the map square, number one colour of cards 1–6 with large letters. Jumble up the second colour and mark A–F making sure that numbers and letters do not correspond e.g 1 might be C, 2–F etc. Laminate the set for repeated use.

Move tables to the side of the room and place the numbered cards on a table at one end and the lettered cards on a table at the other end. Lay them spread apart in a neat row, with numbers and letters easy to read. Each person also needs a piece of paper and a pencil. A sheet of A4 folded to a quarter of its size works well. Write 1–6 as a column and a second column next to it A–F.

Starting from the centre of the room the students can go in either direction back and forth memorising the bits of map and matching the numbers to the letters by drawing lines between them on their sheet of paper until all the cards are matched. They cannot touch or move the cards. First one back at the centre of the room with the two sets correctly matched wins.

A number of sets can be created getting progressively more challenging with more complex ground. Difficulty can also be increased when making the cards, by rotating pieces of map on one set 90 or 180 degrees so that the maps appear different at first glance. The ultimate in this game (not for novice navigators) is to encourage reading of contours and ground shape by making up a set that has map pieces at one end of the room. At the other end of the

Figure 1.10 Map memory cards. In the yellow and orange set the maps have been rotated making it slightly harder.

room, place cards with the equivalent area of map but with contours only (these can be traced neatly). The group all have to go the same way, to the normal map pieces first, before going to the contour-only cards.

Similar card sets can be made with a map symbol on the card at one end and the name of it on the card at the other. Another option is to use photos of a feature with its symbol at the other end, or even a photo of the ground to be matched with a piece of map.

Orienteering maps are good for this game as the colours are obvious tags for memorising the bits of map. Two or three sets of six cards are enough, and certainly the first set should be simple and not have any rotated map pieces. Avoid creating sets of more than six pairs as it becomes too difficult. As a tutor, it can be interesting with youngsters; some will only memorise at one end, some both ends and some will know they have completed the exercise when they have matched five pairs.

Making sets with other scales of map can be introduced at a later stage and may help students get more comfortable with the different scales and symbols as they progress.

Section 2: Developing Navigation Skills

There are three key areas of map reading skills that everyone needs to know before they start on compass skills and venture out on their own.

1. The concept of keeping a map 'set' or 'orientated' to the ground with or without a compass.

2. Knowledge of the symbols including contours and being able to interpret them.

3. Awareness of distance through measuring on the map and on the ground.

Those skills should provide the ability to follow a route along a track or prominent line feature on the map, by thumbing and starting to understand scale, appreciating that a measured distance on the map relates to a distance on the ground and vice versa.

We all get temporarily disorientated but invariably it is when we put the map away for a period of time. Encourage inquisitiveness. Is a feature seen on the map identifiable on the ground and vice-versa? Long periods of walking with no obvious features means people lose concentration – another reason why learning on large-scale maps with lots of information is so good for building confidence.

Map symbols

The classroom ice-breaker puzzle and drawing exercises allow students to start to interpret what they see and make sense of the map symbols. Orienteering map symbols are actually quite intuitive. Historically the theory of the colour on orienteering maps is that terrain is universally uncoloured unless there is more information to add that is useful to the competitor on visibility (yellow - easier navigation and better running speed), or runnability (green - harder navigation and hindrance to running speed).

On other maps one has to interpret the symbols rather more. For instance, every solid black line on a 1:50,000 map is a man-made feature – except for one, the high water mark. The high water mark on the OS 1:25,000 is a thin blue line resembling a stream running around the coast. A black line on either scale usually indicates a fenced boundary but actually it could also be a wall or a hedge. (Field boundaries are marked on OS 1:25,000 but not on 1:50,000).

Look at a forest boundary on an OS 1:50,000 map. It either has a solid black line (a fence) or a small dashed line (see Figure 2.1). This looks like a footpath and has caused much consternation to most hill walkers and many a DofE group who have tried to

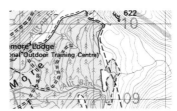

Figure 2.1 Dashed black lines are used to indicate woodland edge and also footpaths on OS 1:50,000 scale mapping.
Map © Ordnance Survey

follow it. These little dashes actually indicate that the wood is unfenced and because trees seed out, the tree line can become quite inaccurate. The same dashes are found along the sides of roads in upland areas of the UK. It does not mean there is a footpath down each side – it is an unfenced road. That is probably one of the most useful pieces of information about symbols for any youth group undertaking an expedition in the hills. Make sure they can recognise the difference between the slightly longer thicker footpath dashes and the unfenced boundary dashes. Then compare with the 1:25,000 scale.

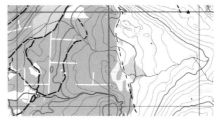

Figure 2.2 The same area as Figure 2.1 on HARVEY 1:40,000 scale mapping. Map © HARVEY

(Orienteering maps use little dotted lines to mark distinctive vegetation changes, so not dissimilar to an OS 1:50,000 map. This provides a progression).

The Key or Legend on most UK maps carries a huge amount of information beyond the simple symbols. It is worth reading and interpreting.

A map reading exercise for an indoor session on a wet day is to choose a grid line on a 1:25,000, 40,000 or 50,000 scale map – ideally projected on a screen so all can see it. Then ask the students in turn to describe walking along the line for one kilometre, maybe two. They have to describe what they should be able to see on their left and right and ahead as they progress along it. This might start off very simply: 'crossed a road, came into a forest' – quite two-dimensional. It could progress though to three dimensions 'crossing the contours diagonally downhill for 250m before crossing the road. After 300m on the flat we come into a fir forest' etc. This really gets people starting to concentrate on the detail. In a larger class this could could get boring though, so keep it lively. Get the last person to select the next person, turn from a North-South grid line to an East-

West one, or an alternative line feature if there are some interesting symbols along it.

Distance, timing and pacing

This topic is appropriate quite soon after an initial map walk, as it helps to gauge the scale. It is easy to grasp, and so builds confidence.

Judging distance

This may be something that comes with age and experience but most young people can quickly gauge the length of a football pitch or 100 metre track and make a reasonable estimate of short distances.

A simple exercise to help gain an appreciation of distance on the ground is to place people or objects in a field or sports ground at say 25m, 50m, 75m and 100m. Question the group as to the distance and see if they can relate the person to the length of a thumb at arm's length at each distance.

Measuring distance and speed

Measuring distance on the map has to be matched by a method of measuring it on the ground. This is done either through pacing or through timing. Both in reality are only 90-95% accurate, so we should not get too concerned as to whether we might have taken 64 or 65 paces whilst dodging around in rough ground.

Timing

Timing can involve all the party but it is not particularly accurate for shorter distances of a few hundred metres. However, remember that we are usually looking for a feature at the end of the measurement. Unlike pacing, timing and measuring distance is a planning tool.

The formula commonly used for working out one's walking speed is 'Naismith's rule'. It is often quoted as 4kph plus 1 minute per 10m of ascent. Downhill is treated the same as the flat. It should really be seen as a guideline, or more precisely, a formula to aid planning and estimating a return time. It identifies a relationship between time, distance and ascent and is often relevant when averaged out over a day's journey. It can be adapted to each group or individual and can provide a mental catching feature to help avoid over-shooting the destination. Everyone can usually keep an eye on the time.

However, the speed of the group is limited by the slowest person, but don't blame them. Neither the slowest nor the fastest person in a group is the problem. The problem is the difference in speed, so compatibility in terms of speed is an issue to be considered. A group with heavy rucsacs going for 8 hours would be wise to plan their journey on around 3kph (20 minutes per km = 2 minutes per 100m) or even less.

The best guide is to under-estimate your speed; everyone hates being rushed at the end of a hard day. During walks the group should come to recognise what is a comfortable speed for the slowest person and then work out the timings based on that, rather than on any theory as to what a group should do. Doing this early in the day allows for plans to be changed and communicated to others at home or meeting the group.

Pacing

Pacing is useful in poor visibility, when the terrain is complex, or if there are several similar features such as paths in a wood. Mountain bikers often create unmarked paths branching off the main track which can confuse the navigator. Pacing is only appropriate for short distances, probably less than 700m. It requires uninterrupted concentration to count. Similar to walking speed, everyone is slightly different. Pacing is commonly used with a bearing aiming across forest or open country, but can be just as valuable for finding, or, for example, helping to determine the first path junction marked on the map from the car park.

Distance travelled	Walking speed			
	5km/hr	4km/hr	3km/hr	2km/hr
1000m	12m	15m	20m	30m
900m	10m 48s	13m 30s	18m	27m
800m	9m 36s	12m	16m	24m
700m	8m 24s	10m 30s	14m	21m
600m	7m 12s	9m	12m	18m
500m	6m	7m 30s	10m	15m
400m	4m 48s	6m	8m	12m
300m	3m 36s	4m 30s	6m	9m
200m	2m 24s	3m	4m	6m
100m	1m 12s	1m 30s	2m	3m

Figure 2.3 Timing table. This can be used a number of ways: as a planning tool before a walk; as a timing tool when on the move; and if you time your pacing over 100m and work out your current speed and re-plan your day, it is a safety management tool

Pacing

- It is more accurate over short distances (200–300m) than timing.

- It provides an appreciation of the map scale, giving a visual picture of it.

- It is simple to teach and understand for both the tutor and the student, helping to build confidence with the map.

- It is useful for simple navigation tasks, like measuring how far along the track to the path junction.

- Recording the time taken to walk 100m of pacing gives a speed of travel which is then a leadership/management decision-making tool, helping to help the group to re-plan the day's journey.

- The most successful navigation teaching methodology in the UK, orienteering, views it as a skill to be taught in the early stages of learning. So does the NNAS.

- In the wider context, pacing was being used very accurately by Alexander the Great around 300BC by specialist pacing troops known as Bematists. The compass appeared nearly 1,500 years later, around 1200AD.

Pacing ought to be introduced on flat ground at an early stage and should not be seen as something that only goes with compass work. Pacing is generally accurate to about 95%. Practice can improve accuracy and remember that one is usually looking for an obvious feature at the end. It provides a mental catching feature.

Measure out 100m on a flat piece of ground and get the group to walk in a relaxed and natural manner back and forth a few times, to work out how many double steps they do to 100m (if they count every step they end up with a lot more). It is easier to choose one foot and count each time that one touches the ground. Most will be around 65 paces but everyone is different. The important thing is consistency. This will only come by using a natural gait.

Once they have a figure for 100m, ask everyone to pace 50m and stop. From the front to the back person the spread should not be more than about 5m (2.5m either side of the 50m mark). This demonstrates that a group average can be useful if more than one person in a group can pace.

Next ask the group to time themselves over a 100m walk then multiply by ten, to work out how long it takes to walk 1km at that speed. They can then calculate how many kilometres per hour that is, i.e. 2 minutes for 100m = 20 minutes per kilometre which = 3 kilometres per hour. This is useful when a group is going slower than planned on a long walk. If the day was planned on 4kph and the group are doing 3kph, it is time to amend the route plan. This is best done earlier rather than later in the day.

Having done the above exercises on a prepared 100m line, go straight onto a map, ideally 1:10,000, and use a real example on the map along a track between two features, ideally 1cm (100m) apart. Measure the distance on the map using a piece of grass to compare it to the scale on the map, or use the compass scale. The group then pace it and should stop when their pacing is done and see where they are in relation to the destination. If this is carefully chosen and tested to be accurate by the tutor it can have a powerful impact on the student and create confidence with the skill.

If pacing for, say, 400 metres it is best to count 4 × 100 metre segments, keeping track of how many 100m have been completed. This is easier than multiplying pacing for 100m by four and counting up to that number. Each 100m can be recorded by picking up a pebble, or starting with four and discarding one at each 100m point. Using fingers, beads, or other people to help, all work fine too.

At a later point, experiment with measuring 100m over rougher ground and up- and downhill. Pacing is not really useable on steep slopes and it is least accurate going downhill. Accuracy depends not only on consistent pacing but also on how accurately the distance is measured on the map. This is compromised on a hill because the map does not represent the actual distance on the ground. 100m measured on a 1:25,000 scale map, where the slope is at an angle of 20 degrees (5mm between index contour lines) measures 106 metres on the ground. At 30 degrees this adds approximately 15m. However by that time pacing becomes irrelevant as we are usually zig zagging up the hill and timing per 100m of ascent becomes a more appropriate measurement tool.

When pacing it is not possible to talk to the group or be interrupted. Using timings, on the other hand, those without technical knowledge can also keep an eye on the time.

Interestingly, a pace usually measures the same as an individuals arm span. Also, in winter one can judge the consistency of one's pace length by the footprint in the snow. A gap of one boot length between the heel of the left footprint and the toe of the right represents walking at normal pace, say 60 paces per 100m. Half a boot length between footprints: add on half again (90 paces); heel to toe means double the number of paces (120) over 100m.

Lastly, pacing is not often needed but when used it is usually in the context of poor visibility or when accurate navigation is important, with or without a compass.

Contours

This is the third dimension and gives us 30% of the information we can get from the map. Largely ignoring contours is denying yourself a massive amount of map information, especially in the hills.

There is a fascinating history behind the development of contours (see section 7 p.44). They are all measured from the high water mark – a black line on the OS 1:50,000 scale which is the only black line on that scale of map that is not a man made feature. The high water mark on the OS 1:25,000 is a thin blue line resembling a stream running around the coast.

There are two elements to this topic. Firstly, understanding what contours represent i.e. the theory behind the lines and shapes. Secondly, how to use and integrate navigation techniques with them.

A contour line joins points of equal height and they do this at intervals usually of 5 or 10 metres above sea level. Every 5th contour we call an index contour and they are shown as thicker lines. (It can be easier to count the index lines instead: 50, 100, 150 etc). On OS maps if the ground becomes very steep, thin contour lines may be omitted but not the index contours. Harvey maps use a 15m contour interval and, on the British Mountain Map, also add colour shading for greater clarity.

On maps containing contour values, when one reads the height numbers, up hill is above the number and streams run downhill in the valleys to bigger rivers or lochs. In winter, contours are often the only source of information we have for navigation, although deep snow can sometimes distort the ground shape.

Orienteering maps also show depressions in the

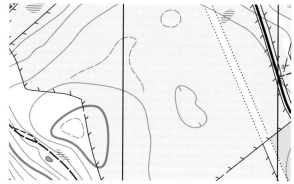

Figure 2.4 Orienteering map extract with contour details shown in brown: a depression (with two small check marks) and form lines (dashed lines). Map © HARVEY

ground using a circular contour but it has check marks on the inside of the contour line ring which point downwards into the middle of the circle. In addition they also use dashed line contours which are known as 'form lines' and give the user a better picture of the ground, indicating that the ground between two contour lines is not a uniform slope for instance. Harvey maps occasionally use an auxiliary contour line in the same way.

Contours require a conceptual understanding as they are not visible on the ground, yet they are the most reliable information on our maps. Contours are the only thing on the map that we can feel (besides walking into water or a tree). We can feel with our eyes shut what the ground is doing under our feet and the relationship our direction of travel has with the imaginary lines. We also learn to visualise the ground shape and steepness. For this reason we need a good range of practical exercises and progressions to build confidence which can help tutors analyse and resolve difficulties that students sometimes experience with this element of navigation.

Introducing and interpreting contours in the classroom

Digital mapping and smart boards are a great asset when teaching contours and ground shape. Most digital mapping packages now offer a 3D fly through facility.

Using a photocopy of a contoured area, the class can try shading in re-entrants and gullies and draw lines down ridges and spurs. This can help to highlight the terrain and make it stand out. They also need to be aware of the height numbers which is often the only way of telling which direction is uphill. With maps that do not have height numbers marked, water features help in determining what is up and down. There are a couple of rules to help:

The rule of Os: a ring-shaped contour is a high piece of ground.

The rule of Vs: if the V points up the hill towards an O then it depicts a gully or re-entrant (often has a stream in it) and if it points away from the ring contours then it is a ridge.

There is a useful quiz sheet resource on the British Orienteering website.

A hand with fingers spread on the table illustrates ridges and valleys. Another similar activity is to draw contours around your knuckles when your hand is in a fist, then flatten your hand. Better still wear a surgical glove and do the same – saves ink on your hands, and flattening a glove has more visual impact being similar to a paper map. You can keep the glove for another time as well.

Ceiling tiles

Using polystyrene tiles, draw a series of individual contour shapes and cut them out with a very sharp blade. When stacked they should produce a hill with features such as a gully, a spur, steep and shallow slopes. A ridge and two summits creates a col as well (keep it to A4 size). Try slicing a small hilltop tile in half to reduce its depth. It could then be used to illustrate a spot height.

Stack them, and by moving them around create steeper or gentle slopes on different aspects. Draw around each layer on a piece of flip chart paper (A1 size) to make a contour map and then write in N, S, E, W around the edge of the sheet to give some context. Students can use labels to help identify features.

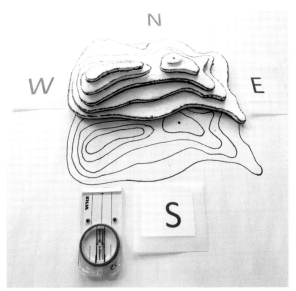

Figure 2.5 A model help to explain contours, topographical features and even slope aspect

tures. The model can be embellished with blue wool for streams, green patches of cloth for woods etc.

A similar exercise is to pile school bags or rucsacs in the middle of the room and put a big sheet over them (which possibly you could draw contours on). Shape it in around the bags to create a range of topographical features. Other materials could create paths and rivers etc.

Identify features that create linear patterns: valleys or re-entrants, ridges, and significant changes in contour spacing, as these can be valuable navigation handrail features on the hill. Lastly introduce the idea of a hillside having an aspect and the possibility of using the compass needle to assist. To help understand the fall line or to visualise it, it may be possible to roll a ping pong ball or marble down an even slope on a model.

Blindfold walk

Use an embankment or reasonably short steep slope with a smooth surface. In pairs, one shuts their eyes, the other is a sighted guide. The sighted guide leads the blind person up, down, diagonally, traversing around on the slope and asks them what is happening with the ground. Swap over to share the experience. Next get the group to place some climbing ropes or thick cord across the hillside to represent two contour lines. Use a ruler or ski stick to give an interval of around half to one metre. Ideally find a bank with an area where the slope changes in steepness (see Figure 2.6). The distance between the ropes should change in that area, creating a strong visual effect for the learner. Encourage them to stand away from the area and at either end to get a better impression of the accuracy of their contour lines. Walk the slope again seeing and thinking about how it feels and what the relationship is between the feeling and the contours.

If no ropes are available then ask the group to spread themselves across the slope and imagine they are standing at the edge of a loch and they just have their toes in the water. They should all end up at the same height across the slope.

Finally with a compass it is possible to give a rough slope aspect just looking at the needle whilst looking down the slope from above the ropes – just an estimation, North East for instance. It helps if the concept was dropped in with the tiles in the classroom (see ceiling tiles on previous page), and, again a ball could be used to help illustrate the concept.

Sand pits

Draw some contour lines (around four is enough) making a simple hill feature on a post card. Make a set of six or so, each one different. Using a sand pit or large trays (cat litter trays are useful) full of damp sand put the class into groups of 2–3. Each has some sand and a contour card. They must now form the hill drawn on the card. String is used to lay around the hill to indicate the contours. Standing up above the model and comparing the string with the diagram is helpful and they can view each other's models. Then swap cards and try another or work it in reverse. Look at someone else's sand hill without the string and draw some contours on a card. Add the string contours and see if they match. Again the concept of slopes having different aspects can be dropped in with the help of a compass needle.

Contour only map walk

This may be quite a difficult exercise to manage as it can be tricky to find a small area with good contour features to create a contour only map. A contour only map is easily made, however, by tracing the contours from a map and then placing them on a sheet of paper.

Include a scale and north south grid lines, so a com-pass needle can be used for orientation. Knolls generally indicate high ground but adding numbers for contours, even if they are only symbolic, may help. Draw a route on the map, in and out, and up and down contour features. Each person has a map and the tutor leads a map walk following the line on the map and pointing out the contour features and focusing on the contours and how they feel and look. If you have a relatively private piece of wood, you can put tape ribbons in the trees to mark the route and small markers at obvious features.

See chapter 7 for resources for teaching contours.

Other map reading exercises

Further map walks bringing together the skills covered so far are a good way of getting out and building confidence and knowledge. Use line features such as streams which appear to be going more cross-country, rather than following paths. Look for features just off the chosen line feature being followed. Start to cut corners between line features, across country. Look at ground shape to help with contour interpretation, and introduce simple processes of relocation (setting the map with and without compass, matching the ground to the map, and the notion of aiming off (see page 35).

Figure 2.6 Making contours.

Try exercises to develop confidence and independence. Use questions such as "what is coming up next on the right or left?" "how far to the next feature?" and then measure it on the ground. Identify tick-off features and catching features. Take it in turns amongst the group to lead, with and without telling the group what the destination is. With a small group give each person a point to stop at along a track, the furthest one goes off first. When the last one has set off, the tutor follows up checking each one has stopped at the right place and sets the next point to go to. They end up leapfrogging along the path but they are navigating independently.

Going in pairs or solo

Beware of setting out a longer navigation route around linear features in an orienteering style challenge similar to a Bronze NNAS assessment, and then allowing the students the option to choose to visit checkpoints in any order. This can become a bit of a disaster, as they will have a tendency to head to the point that appears easiest, or is on the biggest feature, but after that are off the line features without the knowledge to travel in the right direction, cross-country, to it, and without the knowledge of aiming off. They will have limited experience of relocating on a linear feature and working out a strategy should they have the possibility of being on one of several similar line features.

If a checkpoint is at a junction – a path or fence for instance, place a marker a few metres along the feature you want them to follow in order to help create a successful confidence building outcome. Placing a marker at the most convenient place for you, because there is a tree to hang it on for instance, could leave too much choice or even be misleading for the enthusiastic competitive students!

The bottom line is to match the challenge to what has been taught. The structure of teaching and colour coded courses that orienteers use is really helpful in understanding this and is outlined in section 6 as a useful reference.

Grid references

Consider why and when to teach this subject and how important is it to the teaching of navigation? In reality grid references are very rarely used when navigating. They are about communicating a location to

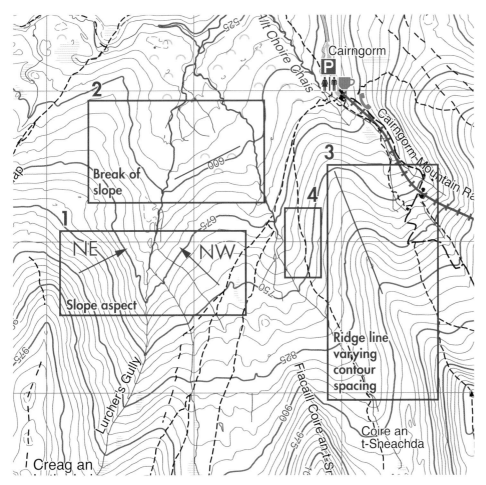

Figure 2.7 Contours create topographical features which we can not only see but feel underfoot

1. Contours give us a slope aspect (the direction the slope faces)

2. Break of slope (change of steepness) can provide a linear feature

3. Ridge Line – the changes in contour spacing provide tick off and catching features on an existing line feature

4. Heading south the path gently crosses the contours then parallels the contour line for 200m so is flat, then steepens again and starts to cross the contours at right angles. In 3km along this path this is the only point at which it runs flat

All these changes can be felt as well as seen

Map © HARVEY

another person. If a student on a DofE expedition called the supervisor to say they had a problem the supervisor would have a good idea of the route and roughly where the team should be so a location description may be all that is required.

Good map reading skills on the move should be the first skills to develop. However, it is appreciated that grid references have to be taught at some point before people head into the hills. For many they are a part of route cards. However, they could be first taught separately from navigation in a session on safety, by tying it into telephoning to get picked up, or for an emergency.

There are several approaches to teaching grid references. Keep it as simple as possible. Avoid the big picture science behind map making and grids. Remember a description should always go with a grid.

If one searches online for "Teaching Grid References" there are a host of ideas and resources.

Start with four-figure references then move to six-figures. Students can estimate a six-figure grid by eye. So long as they are roughly right that is fine. They will be accurate enough, especially if a descrip-

tion is added. Later they can explore the accuracy obtainable with a ruler or the scales on the compass (sometimes known as a romer).

Another approach could be to see if students can learn it on their own from the key on an OS or Harvey map. It is all explained there, but people tend not to read it.

Figure 2.9 is an example of a grid sheet to help get the idea without too much clutter. It helps to reduce confusion. Every student should have a copy. Then it is easy to ask for a grid reference for point A. Trying to get a class to all find the same point on a map is usually where problems start, adding complexity to what is a simple exercise. The common starting point tends to be learning the sequence "along the corridor and up the stairs" – along the bottom numbers and then up the side numbers, or E (east) comes before N (north) in the alphabet. Once they have got the concept on the sheet it is easy to move to a map.

Digital mapping on a smart board makes it easier for everyone to see the point selected for a grid reference. Lastly if the mapping is available, each person can see what is produced by using their date of birth as a six-figure grid reference.

Figure 2.8 Grid references should be taught at some point before people head into the hills on their own

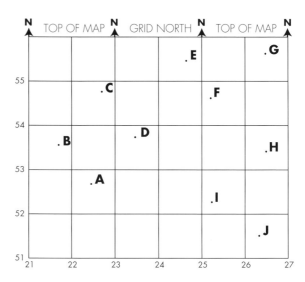

Figure 2.9 Teaching grid references. This form of diagram makes it quick to identify a place – a letter as opposed to a symbol on the map that may take some students a while to find and of which there may be a quite a few on the map. Also cheaper to ensure everyone has a map. Along the corridor then up the stairs, 'E' comes before 'N' so go east then north

Section 3: Teaching Compass Skills

Introduction

When to introduce the compass provides an interesting debate and is something that tutors can experiment with. Some research in Sweden suggested that introducing a compass (just the needle for map setting) from almost the first map walk helps associate the map and compass together. It builds confidence with the device and those who had used the compass from the start appeared to pick up more complex skills more quickly than those who were introduced to the compass only when taking bearings became a relevant skill.

Using a simple compass with just a needle, so there is no distraction with a rotating dial or baseplate, enables a useful progression to a standard walker's compass. However, it may seem an additional expense on top of a compass for the hills. A simple needle-only compass can also be quite a powerful teaching tool when working with adults who have learned some traditional compass skills in the past and try to over-complicate the processes.

Map setting with a compass

There are several ways of doing this. One is to grasp the compass baseplate in one hand, the map in the other and simply bring the map in underneath the compass needle. Align the needle to the top of the map along the N, S grid lines, either by turning your whole body or by turning the map. Another method is to simply lay a compass onto the map, rotate the whole map with the compass lying on it and watch the red end of the needle until it points to the top of the map where the title would be. (The needle should be parallel to the north south grid lines or the side of the map). The map is then set. It should not take more than three seconds and there is no need to even touch the compass, let alone turn the housing dial or align the baseplate in any way.

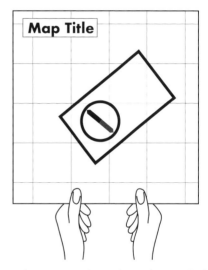

Figure 3.3a The compass is dropped onto the map; the body, map and compass are rotated as one

Figure 3.1 Simple compasses

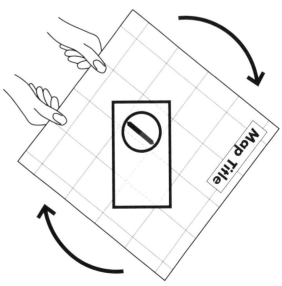

Figure 3.3b Map is set: the floating needle points to the top of the map and there is no need to turn the compass housing or align the base plate

Figure 3.2 Thumb compass typically used by orienteers

Challenge the group to walk around their maps keeping them set with the needle always pointing up to the title.

Once the map is set the compass could be put away, but keeping the compass held on the edge of the map enables one to grip the two items together and keep the map set at-a-glance without the compass obscuring the map. This is a useful habit to encourage as it saves time and helps maintain contact between the ground and the map.

Figure 3.4 Map setting with compass on the side of the map

The baseplate compass
The baseplate compass is often introduced with a mass of information that is beyond the learner's comprehension. However, at some point, ideally after map setting is grasped, it will be helpful to define the parts of the compass for ease of teaching and a common language. Confusion between the needle and arrows is a common cause of problems. Tutors should be very careful not to muddle the terms.

Compass tips
A compass is a scientific instrument and should be cared for. It could be a life-saver in the hills and therefore it is worth investing in a good one. Consider renewing it every 5–10 years.

The Silva Mk 4 or one of the Suunto A-30 range are examples of good hill compasses with a long baseplate, a magnifier and a variety of measuring scales. A compass with 1:40,000 scale makes working with some Harvey maps of that scale much easier. Currently only the Silva Mk 4 expedition has this on.

Keep it well away from smartphones. These devices

Figure 3.5 Base plate compasses

in particular have a strong magnet in the speaker and it does not make any difference whether they are switched on or not. The magnet can permanently change the polarity of a compass and it will need to be returned to the manufacturer. Unfortunately a compass and phone are rather similar in shape and can both end up rubbing together in a pocket or lid of a rucsac. Also check the magnetism of other items: radios and digital cameras often have small speakers in them. Some drinking tubes attach to rucsacs with magnets. Belt buckles, and even mitts that can be turned into fingerless gloves use magnets to keep things in place. While a magnet can permanently change the polarity, a piece of metal with iron in it, and items such as a GPS, may deviate the needle if they are close by.

A magnifying glass is useful for fine detail.

The millimetres on the side of the compass are for accurately measuring distance. 1mm = 50m on a

Figure 3.6 Reverse polarity

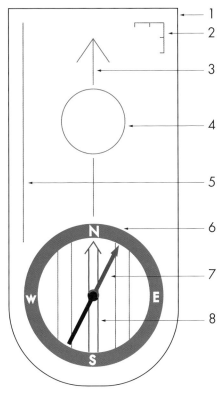

1 Base Plate
2 Romer
3 Direction of travel arrow
4 Magnifer
5 Use this inner line instead of the compass edge for taking bearings
6 Compass housing, dial or capsule
7 Magnetic Needle
8 Orientating lines and arrow to align with north - south lines on the map

Figure 3.7 Compass terminology

1:50,000 map. Because the millimetres are marked on the underside of the plastic baseplate, reading them off through the side wall of the plastic can make it easier to read.

The length of cord usually supplied with a compass is too short when knotted as a loop, and encourages people to hang the compass around their neck. This is a serious barrier to effective use of the map and compass, even for setting as described in Section 2. Use the cord singly, attaching one end to the compass, the other to your jacket (often the breast pocket zip is used). This will enable the compass to be held in any position and enhance navigation accuracy. Alternatively, double the length of the cord then make a loop and that will go over a head and shoulder and will enable the compass to go in any pocket. Orienteers use a much shorter loop and attach the compass to a wrist, so it is constantly to hand and kept on the map speeding up their navigation.

Figure 3.8 Ready to navigate, map and compass easily to hand

The application of compass bearings

Progression for teaching compass bearings

There are three easy steps for teaching bearings:

1. **Needle only** – Starting with map setting, and ignoring the baseplate and dial, using just the red end of needle pointing to the top of the map. A rough direction can also be gained from this e.g. a north easterly direction.

2. **Needle and base plate only** – Using the base plate on the map aligned along the chosen direction of travel, ignore the dial but align the needle to the top of the map by turning your whole body with map and compass locked together directly in front of you. This is sometimes referred to as a quick, rough or simple bearing yet when aiming down the direction of travel arrow it is remarkably accurate. We will refer to it as a 'quick' bearing here.

3. **Needle, base plate and dial** – Lastly, do 2, as above, and now include turning the dial until the lines and arrow on the bottom of the capsule align to the map's north–south grid lines and the red end of the needle points to the N on the dial, sometimes referred to as putting 'Red Fred in his bed or shed'. The bearing is read off from the direction-of-travel arrow on the baseplate. Keeping everything aligned, follow that arrow. The compass can be removed from the map and used independently from it. This is sometimes referred to as the Silva 1-2-3 system or an accurate, traditional, fine or even recorded bearing. We will refer to it as a 'fine' bearing.

In reality there is little difference in the accuracy between a quick and a fine bearing once you start walking, and both methods work with pacing.

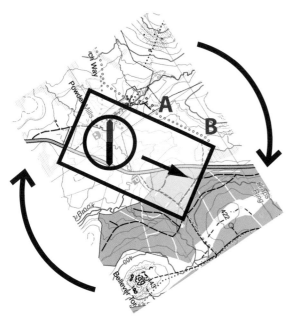

Figure 3.9a Quick bearing. The compass baseplate is aligned along the route to be followed, A-B. Map © HARVEY

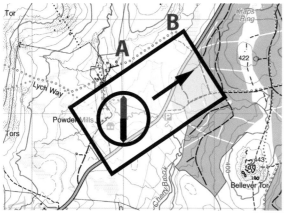

Figure 3.9b Quick bearing. The map and compass together are then orientated to magnetic north, with the compass base plate and direction of travel arrow pointing in the direction of the route to be followed. Map © HARVEY

A quick bearing provides an excellent and simple progression for learning compass work. It is an extension of the map setting process and does not require any turning of the housing capsule. This is all that Bronze DofE, Bronze NNAS, Lowland Leader Award, or Level 2 mountain bike award candidates require.

Two things help manage the teaching of these skills. First is having the map folded into an easily manageable A5 size so it can be held from any side with the compass in the middle of the map. Second, when using the compass for direction, learn to hold it directly in front with the baseplate pointing straight out from the tummy. For novices it may help to hold the edges of the compass baseplate in both hands with the map underneath. The map will usually be at

an odd angle which can initially create a bit of confusion for the learner, but it is set. Lock the wrists and lock elbows into the side, forming a triangle with the forearms in front of the body.

To get the needle to point to the top of the map the only thing that should move is your feet, taking little 'penguin steps' to get the needle to align to the top of the map. Eventually people will just hold the map and compass with one hand in front, and start to bring it up to eye-level to help with accurate aiming.

Quick bearing in detail

With the map folded to the area required, ensure the compass baseplate is the correct way around, place the edge of it, or the inner line, along the desired path or direction on the map. Keeping the compass firmly held on the map with both hands, align the needle to the top of the map by simply turning the body with little steps until the needle comes around to point to the top of the map where the title would be. Body alignment with the compass is crucial.

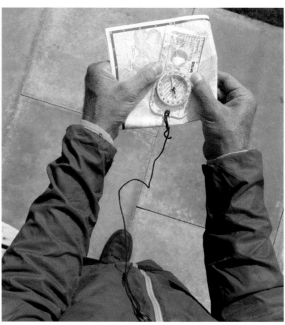

Figure 3.10 Holding the map and compass together with both hands directly in front of your body, with the needle pointing to the top of the map

Look up along the baseplate. It should be pointing straight along the required direction of travel. This is often a lightbulb moment for people. They have just effectively taken a bearing aligning the needle with the N-S grid lines but without turning the dial. If the compass is removed from the map the bearing will be lost, unless a mental note has been made of where the red end of the needle is pointing on the compass dial. That will be different for everyone in the group but does allow the compass to be removed or the bearing recovered should the compass slip on the map.

This is how orienteers navigate, often using a compass with a combination of coloured segments and dots around the edge of the dial instead of numbers. It is extremely effective yet almost unknown in the walking fraternity. It saves time in dial turning and alignment which also reduces the opportunity to make the common 180 degree error often made when turning the dial. (However it is still possible to put the compass on the map the wrong way around, or align the needle to the wrong end of the map).

There is another advantage for hillwalkers of knowing about a quick bearing. It is invaluable when it is difficult to turn the dial for a fine bearing. Reasons for this range from really cold fingers, to wearing thick gloves or mittens, or the underside of the compass dial gripping a rubberised map case too well. In winter it can be a combination of all three!

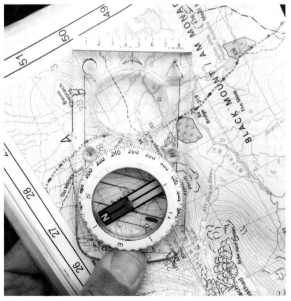

Figure 3.11 Baseplate of compass aligned along chosen direction of travel, with the needle pointing towards the top of the map

Fine bearing in detail

Fine bearings should be taught after quick bearings have been understood and practised. Fine bearings are necessary when there is a requirement to inform others of the exact direction of travel or where/when magnetic variation becomes significant. In the hills when covering large distances over a long period of time, it is more comfortable to separate the map and compass so a fine bearing is often appropriate.

Before doing a fine bearing it is always worth estimating the direction that should end up being

recorded, so if an error in the process is made it will be obvious.

Fine bearings require one step to be added to the quick bearing: turning the compass capsule so that the N on the capsule points to the top of the map aligning the lines on the bottom of the capsule with the N-S grid lines. Follow the process for the quick bearing with the baseplate along the route to be followed and the red end of the needle pointing to the top of the map. Keeping the map and compass steady and set, turn the capsule until the N on the dial also points to the top of the map. The needle will appear lined up inside the arrow on the bottom of the capsule, and the thin lines on the capsule will be aligned with the grid lines on the map. The bearing is read off the dial where the direction of travel arrow on the baseplate starts.

When people are familiar with this it will be apparent that the map setting or needle alignment can be done at the end of the process with the compass off the map.

Turning the capsule makes the compass into a protractor and it retains the bearing and direction of travel so long as the red end of the needle is aligned to the N and the capsule arrow. Aiming and travelling cross-country using pacing or timing can all be added to complete the skill.

Compass manufacturers rate a standard hill compass needle as having up to a 2.5 degree error. The dial is marked in 2-degree graduations and currently magnetic variation is less than 2 degrees. Add to that minor inaccuracies of our base plate, dial and needle alignment and aiming of the compass there is a lot of scope for minor error. When we start actually walking on the bearing all really fine tuning is questionable. Hence in reality there tends to be no difference in accuracy between a quick and a fine bearing.

Magnetic variation

In the UK in 2018 magnetic variation from true-north is around 1.6 degrees west of grid north and decreasing to 0 degrees over the next 10 years, after which going east of grid north. So the old rhyme "Mag to grid get rid, grid to mag add" will no longer be relevant.

In other countries magnetic variation might be an issue, but teaching it can be left until that time comes, rather than adding confusion at the learning stage. Using a reasonably up-to-date orienteering map when learning and practising bearings has the advantage that the lines on it are drawn to magnetic north, so the issue need never arise.

So, simply, if the compass can be kept on the map, there is no need to turn the dial; just rely on the needle pointing to the top of the map. If accuracy in poor weather with careful aiming is required, a bearing needs to be communicated to others in the group, or a magnetic variation adjustment is required, it may be necessary to turn the dial and then the compass can be separated from the map.

If one is using a fine bearing with the compass off the map, it is possible to carry out a quick bearing (perhaps to check the direction of a stream or path) without losing the original fine bearing. In effect one can operate using two bearings on the one compass.

Tools to help teach bearings

We now have a process of teaching that should be easy to comprehend, progressing from map setting, to a quick bearing, to a fine bearing.

All too often the compass is introduced in the classroom at a later stage of learning to navigate. The teaching starts with how to take a bearing on a large-scale map for walking cross country from point A to point B (but without then actually going outside and doing it). There is no context or way to recognise a successful outcome. Grid references are also often used to identify point A and B and this creates a feeling that the task is complex and difficult before it has even started.

Since much of the training in navigation is done with the aim of young people undertaking a walking expedition through the countryside rather than over the mountains, the most common use of a bearing is to confirm at a junction which path to take. So here are some exercises to get to that understanding and help develop compass skills.

Classroom quick bearings

On a computer make up a diagram similar to Figure 3.12 as an A4 size sheet in landscape orientation. Give each student a copy. Fold the sheet in half so it is easier to handle. Set the scenario that: "you are at the junction A with a choice of tracks on the ground. Your plan from the map was to go to B". Normally setting the map would determine the correct path. However if more assurance is required a quick bearing can be appropriate. Place the edge of the compass (or the inner line) between A and B with the baseplate pointing in the direction of travel, stand

up with the compass on the map, get behind the compass (elbows locked in and hands superglued together) with it firmly in place on the map. Turn around (penguin steps) until the needle comes around to point to the top of the map. Check the general direction is right. In the room, on looking up, everyone should be facing the same way. Keep repeating with different legs and increase the speed as the students become more confident.

The common issue at this stage is people holding the compass at an odd angle in front of them. They have to ignore the map and focus just on the compass needle and keeping the compass pointing straight ahead of them. As their nose points out from their face so should the compass point straight out from their tummy.

Classroom fine bearings

Figure 3.12 also works well for introducing traditional bearings at a later stage. Estimate the bearing before turning the capsule to help eliminate the classic 180° error. To build confidence and get the idea that it really is a very simple process, speed it up, going randomly from letter to letter. Usually

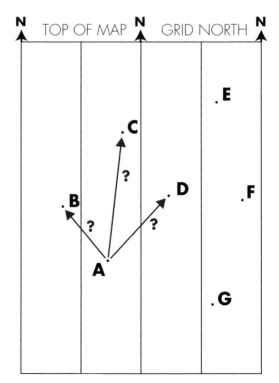

Figure 3.12 Teaching bearings. When introducing bearings it is about simplifying the process of using the compass and route choice, not travelling cross-country hence starting with the "which track is it A, B, or C?" idea. Enlarged to A4, this sheet also allows the learner to focus quickly on the compass without the need for grid references to identify points on the map indoors

someone will end up facing the rest of the group. Can they work out what has happened? (180° error as a result of the compass being the wrong way around on the map, or the dial turned with the N pointing to the south end of the map. Worryingly, if both errors are made the student will be facing the same way as everyone else and the bearing will be correct!)

Outdoor exercises: bearings cards

These cards can be used for a number of exercises, from developing an understanding of the cardinal points with or without a compass, to teaching bearings (see page 10). They provide small progressions and can be done anywhere there is space. The only reservation is that it can end up introducing numbers, angles and bearings, and jumping to the accurate bearing process too quickly.

The cards provide a link from classroom bearing exercises to going outdoors with a map. They enable the tutor to build confidence with the compass for the learners, and be on hand immediately if there are any difficulties.

Set-up

The circles on the cards represent nine markers which can be laid out using chalk on tarmac or a gym floor, or indicated by placing cones on a flat area of grass. Plastic sports marker cones are good, but you can use anything you have ten of.

Lay out nine cones on the ground as accurately as possible, with the design properly orientated to magnetic north. Around ten steps between each cone works well. They must make a symmetrical square. (This is a slightly different set up from the 9-cone map setting exercises).

Clearly identify north on the ground by marking a large N on the 10th cone. Place that cone at the north end to correspond with the N on the cards. A large N can also be marked on each of the 3 cones of the northern row.

Explanation

Bring the group to the south end, each person with a diagram card. Doing this seems to make it easier to understand when explaining the layout. Give the group a little while to identify the cones and get an understanding of the layout – the four sides, each of three cones, are North, East, South and West. Split the group into pairs to work together.

The exercises

Quick bearings

From any corner pairs first identify where they are standing and then simply place the compass edge (or inner baseplate line) on the map along from their corner circle to the next circle (an option of 5 in the diagram shown). Then, holding the compass with both hands on the sides, and keeping the compass still aligned on the map with the baseplate pointing straight ahead of them, they simply turn their bodies

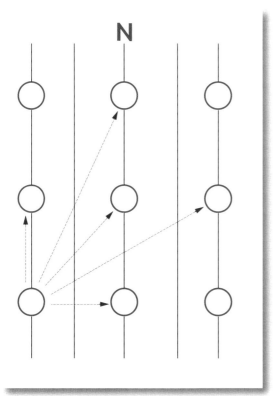

Figure 3.13 Map for 9 cones laid out as a square to introduce quick bearings

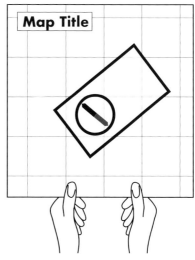

Figure 3.14 FIgure 3.3a (p25) is repeated here for convemience

until the needle points to the top of the map where the N is. At this point the map becomes set.

This is often the lightbulb moment. There is a sudden realisation that, with the needle pointing to the top of the map, they find that the direction of travel arrow along the baseplate points to exactly the cone they want to go to. Folding a map down to a small size where the thumbs can more or less reach the centre of the map becomes useful. (People who have previously been taught to take bearings in the traditional manner find it very difficult not to turn the dial and try to get the needle aligned with the housing capsule arrow and taking the compass off the map. Undoing this habit keeps the tutor busy)!

People can choose to remain at the corner and aim for different cones or they can walk it. In the end if pairs have a pen they can mark the card with a route of about 5 legs around the cones for their partner to navigate around using quick bearings. This process is accurate and simple and it creates a progression towards the fine bearing. It also illustrates that a fine bearing can add unnecessary complications and takes longer.

Once people are happy with the process, it is ideal to use an orienteering map and apply quick bearings to every linear feature they come across e.g. paths, streams, fences, edge of woods etc. They may appre-ciate that, in confirming these line features from map to ground, they are carrying out a simple relocation skill. From that, progress to short cross-country legs within the park or grounds to re-enforce the process. Keeping the map folded small is a great help.

Accurate bearings

At a later stage in developing navigators, the cones can be put out again and the traditional method taught which allows the compass to be removed from the map.

The quick bearing still works if the compass is removed from the map but one has to make a mental note of where the red end of the needle is pointing on the dial (which will be different for everyone), or lastly to turn the dial and carry out a fine bearing.

In turning a quick bearing into a fine one, it may help to describe turning the dial as a means of simply 'recording' the bearing.

Other exercises

Use a set of small cards with different lists of basic directions (see example in Figure 3.16): one card per pair or individually. **Ensure the group understands that these directions are just to the next nearest marker and that if they get it right they should end up where they started.** The compass can be

Figure 3.15 Quick bearings using a square nine-cone layout

START NE CORNER

*One cone at a time,
finish where you started.*

Leg 1 – head **South**
Leg 2 – head **West**
Leg 3 – head **South**
Leg 4 – head **East**
Leg 5 – head **North West**
Leg 6 – head **North East**

Basic directions

START SW CORNER

*One cone at a time,
finish where you started.*

Leg 1 – head **0°**
Leg 2 – head **90°**
Leg 3 – head **315°**
Leg 4 – head **90°**
Leg 5 – head **180°**
Leg 6 – head **225°**

Compass bearing directions

Figure 3.16 Basic direction cards

used just to remind students of the relationship between N, S, E and W. (They should ignore the baseplate and needle at this point).

The second card with bearing numbers may not be an appropriate exercise until a later date, due to the introduction of numbers and turning the dial.

Walking on the bearing

This is an exercise to develop the understanding of sighting with the compass and walking accurately on a bearing. Put the group in pairs and choose a starting point, such as a tree. One person takes a bearing with their compass on an object say 50–100m away (a cone or post). This can be done as a quick bearing by noting the exact position of the red end of the needle against a number on their dial, or a fine bearing by keeping the needle aligned to the capsule arrow. Then ask them not to look up but just to concentrate on walking on the bearing without aiming on intermediate things or the target object. Use a woolly hat or hood pulled down over their eyes ensuring they can only see down to their feet and compass. They must try to walk to the object with a sighted partner following silently behind ensuring they do not walk into anything.

What should happen is that, because they cannot aim at anything on the ground, they drift to one side. (If they are walking diagonally across a slope the exercise will have more obvious results). When level with the objective remove the hat/hood. Hopefully they will get the idea that they have to navigate by

sighting or aiming with the compass even on small boulders, patches of grass etc. Now ask them to turn around and aim their compass back at the start point by just allowing the white South end of the needle to point to the N on the housing. Depending on how accurately they managed to walk, the direction of travel arrow on the baseplate may not be pointing back to the start. If they now move left or right towards their initial objective it all begins to line up. This is a useful checking system for keeping on a bearing in future journeys on the hill.

Star navigation exercise using the compass

The next stage might be a star event, similar to the map setting star exercise in the first section. It could be in the grounds, a park or a forest. Individuals have a marked orienteering map, an object to be placed out on the ground and a compass. Using a quick bearing they navigate to a feature marked on their map by the tutor, leave their marker and return to the central start point. They then swap maps around in the group and go out using a quick bearing to collect a marker. It does not really matter if on the initial legs they can see where they are going. It confirms the skills and develops sighting with the compass on the map and trusting it. The legs can be gradually made a little more challenging, similar to the star exercises in Section 1, moving the marker to a new position rather than back to the centre etc. Pacing could also be added in if appropriate.

Compass courses

Creating a compass course is a good way to bring bearings and pacing together as a part of building confidence with compass skills. It can be done for both types of bearing.

In a wood, using compass and pacing work out a

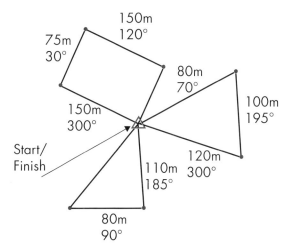

Figure 3.17 Clover leaf compass courses

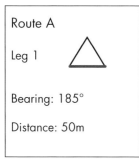

Figure 3.18 A typical board with directions for each leg of a compass course

series of routes with three or four legs all starting from the same point, creating a clover leaf pattern (see Figure 3.17). Ideally this should be close to home as it can take some time to create. Markers can be left out attached to trees semi-permanently. At each change of direction place a board with a laminated instruction card with the leg, bearing and distance. See Figure 3.18. Having the boards on the 'back' of a tree, facing away from the approach direction, can add to the challenge and encourage accuracy of pacing and aiming with the compass.

For a quick-bearing exercise the bearing in degrees is not required. Instead make up cards about A5 size as accurately as possible so each leg of the route matches the bearing but only the distance is given in metres. The student then aligns the compass with the leg on the card and moves until the needle points to the north end of the card and aligns with the grid lines. They then just pace the distance walking on the bearing. See Figure 3.19.

For a fine bearing there is no need for the card. They simply have all the information on the board at each tree and merely put the bearing described onto the compass, aim and pace the distance.

The clover leaf pattern enables the tutor to observe a number of students. If anyone gets lost they can easily return to the centre. Three individuals or pairs can set off at once.

If the courses are laid out on a slope then the pacing can become more challenging.

This exercise can be done with linear routes but the disadvantages are that getting lost means returning to the start, it is hard for the tutor to monitor and lastly the students are able to follow each other.

An alternative compass course exercise

This is another similar exercise which works well on a lawn or sports pitch. It requires laminated cards, marker pens (per-pair) and some sets of 3–4 same-coloured golf tees. (Golf tees come in packs of 20 in four colours). Divide the class into a number of groups according to how many different colours of tee are available. Each group should have a different colour.

Each group chooses an obvious feature (tree) and then, with a bearing and paces, puts out two or three golf tees to make a triangle or square back to the start point. (Keep the distances short and simple, around 50m and don't bury the golf tees). The bearing and distance for each leg are recorded on their card. See Figure 3.20. Now give the marked-up card to a different group to try to follow the route. They will need to aim, choosing intermediate points like a daisy or different coloured patch of grass, and pace carefully to find the tees. Keep swapping the cards around until everyone has had a few goes.

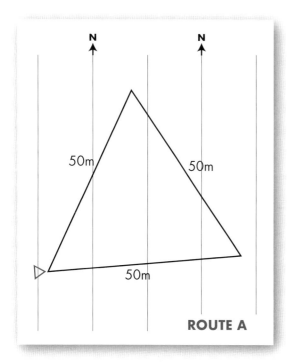

Figure. 3.19 A quick bearing card

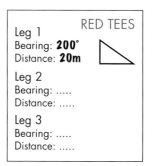

Figure. 3.20 Using golf tees to create compass course

Bearings cross-country

The process can be extended with a map walk on an orienteering map, using quick bearings cross-country, aiming with the compass, and pacing. Try short legs – only 50m to 100m – to find something off to the side of the line feature (an old ruin perhaps or a stream junction). It does not matter if the students can see the objective to begin with. In fact it gives instant feedback that they have got the process correct as they look up from the map. Keep it simple to foster success.

Before moving onto longer cross-country legs ensure that other strategies are in place, such as recognising catching features, aiming off, attack points and relocation skills (see page 38). These mean that if they miss the objective they can work out where they are and successfully find it. Then transfer to maps that have progressively less information.

There are a number of different progressions in this section which can be done with or without turning the dial for a fine bearing. You probably won't use all of them but they should enable a flexible approach depending on time available, map resources, student tutor-ratios etc.

Figure. 3.21 Navigation in misty conditions requires confident use of the compass

Section 4: Navigation Strategies

Most people teaching navigation will be familiar with these strategies and, with an orienteering map in particular, it is easy to provide examples to practise each one several times in a session and develop an understanding and confidence with them. Some skills such as 'boxing' can even be introduced on a playing field with a rope representing a marsh or cliff edge, but confidence with bearings will be required for that particular strategy, so it is likely to be introduced later in the progressions.

There is evidence that experienced navigators tend to plan by working back from the destination to their current location. They first look for possible attack points and catching features, then handrails to link their position to the attack point. Within the leg, other strategies such as aiming off may come into play.

From the beginning of teaching navigation ask simple questions around the destination and how are we going to find it, what do we expect to see, how will we know if we have passed it, how will we know we are getting near it, can we identify tick-off features as we work back to our current location. This introduces the strategies and supports the idea of starting at the destination. Starting from your current location, formulating a plan sometimes takes several attempts, as one gets so far and then realises that a particular route won't quite work. Often a plan is simple and quick but the diagram at 4.2 shows a complex range of choices and potential strategies.

Break down navigation legs

The length of a navigation leg is often dictated by the visibility and whether you are following a linear handrail feature or heading across open country. Poor visibility calls for shorter legs and it is helpful to choose a route offering plenty of detail on the map. In good visibility, where one can see obvious large features several kilometres ahead, navigation can be managed with longer legs and less map detail along the route. This is one reason why orienteering maps are so helpful in learning the skills and building confidence through practice, because in a forest one is effectively operating in poor visibility, which provides the most challenging navigation conditions.

However, the more one is able to break a long leg down into small chunks the more engagement there is with the map and the less chance of becoming disorientated.

It is often the case that, having completed your plan, the first part of a route may be easy along a path, then perhaps following a stream to one of several small junctions which might be referred to as an 'attack point', from which a bearing for a short distance to an isolated point like a col is required. The first part is easy along the track to the stream, the second part to the stream junction will need more care to get the right junction, and third part needs concentration and accuracy with the compass and maybe pacing. It can be interpreted as adopting a traffic light system. As you go through green, orange,

Figure 4.1 Navigating in mountainous terrain brings its own rewards

red, the detail and accuracy required increases. Orienteers also use this in terms of their running speed when navigating this sort of leg.

Catching features

'Catching features' and 'collecting features' are often used to mean the same thing. Although there are two explanations here, it doesn't really matter what they are called. A catching feature is usually something recognised when planning a leg that lies beyond the target; it is a back-stop. If the walker overshoots an objective, the catching feature should provide the warning of having over shot. It could be a clear line feature such as a stream. A change in slope aspect or steepness might be more of a winter feature. An obvious example is heading towards the top of a hill in poor visibility and then finding yourself starting to go downhill. Lastly, timing and pacing provide a mental catching feature. Having estimated a distance from the map, transfer that to the ground and when your pacing or timing is up, stop, check your likely position and create a plan. Often it is to go just a little further. 10% of the original distance is a reasonable measure. Effectively the mental catching feature is moved forwards slightly, to manage the error, but the catching feature should finally stop you going any further.

Physical and mental catching features can be introduced from the start of navigating. The fence around the grounds is often the first catching feature novices understand. During early map walks the idea can be introduced and become a part of the conversation about each leg. At the stage of following line features the objectives are themselves clear catching features e.g. a path junction.

Tick-off features

These are sometimes also referred to as 'collecting' features, and again are points that should be identified at the planning stage or in the hills and are often identified through constant ground-to-map and map-to-ground observations. They help the navigator keep track of their progress towards the target, collecting or ticking off features as they pass them.

Aiming off

This is when one is aiming for a particular point on a linear feature generally running across the direction of travel. Imagine being 500 metres from a river which has a small bridge on it and visibility is poor. Using a compass bearing one aims for the bridge and arrives at the river but then cannot see the bridge. It is difficult to decide which way to turn

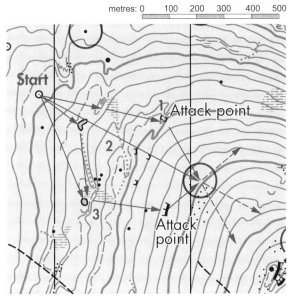

Figure 4.2 Attack points and catching features. Map © HARVEY

along the river. The solution is not to aim at the bridge in the first place. Aim off to one side of the bridge by 5-10% of the overall distance, and when the river is reached it is simple to know which way to turn to find the bridge.

Attack point

An attach point is a feature that is bigger and more obvious than the final destination feature. This is used when the target is say 800m away across country, and may be difficult to find. 800m on a bearing with pacing may be a risky strategy. If there is a clearly recognisable feature closer to the target (say 300m away) which can be guaranteed to be found, go to that first to reduce the potential percentage error. A common error is to choose attack points that are smaller than the target.

Choosing an attack point may dictate the catching feature or change a mental one, such as pacing, into a physical one, such as a fence. Stream heads are often not particularly well marked on maps, and using the mental catching feature of pacing up a stream accurately for say 800m and determining the end of it, can be tricky at the best of times. An attack point off to one side of the stream head, perhaps a small knoll 300m to one side requiring a dog leg route, could mean that the catching feature becomes the ground dipping and rising as the stream bed is crossed. Chances are that using the attack point, with a second short leg and a physical catching feature, will be more accurate and easier to execute.

An orienteering map with line features and features such as a boulders along them, or a junction, will provide many opportunities for practice. At some point it will become obvious that one can aim directly at a right-angle path junction and on arriving at a path with the map set, immediately determine which side of the junction you are on by the alignment of the path. This is relying on relocation on a line feature rather than aiming off, but both achieve the same thing in this scenario.

Figure 4.2 clearly illustrates some of the possible options on a navigation leg up a slope. Start the plan from the destination and work back to your starting point. The key things are an attack point and identifying a catching feature, which could be a change in slope angle (physical) or pacing (mental). These two things are interlinked. Route choice 3 using the southernmost pond and a cliff as tick-off feature and attack point is the only route that has a catching feature that would almost immediately indicate you have overshot the target. You would find yourself paralleling the contours, whereas the other alternatives you would feel no change in the slope beyond the objective. The route may be longer but one can handrail the re-entrant between the ponds and there is a boulder between the pond and the outcrop as a tick off feature: all much more re-assuring. Using straight-line bearings tends to lead to a 'navigate to relocate' approach and the problem is relocation is the weakest technique for many.

Boxing or dog-legs

This is a strategy that merely needs good confidence with a compass and measuring skills on the map and the ground. It can be tried with a large-scale map around corners of building and features in a school grounds before being taken into the limited visibility of a forest area or even tried at night. It is used to avoid an obstacle – corrie rim or marsh for instance. Imagine heading due north and coming to a cliff edge. One could go due west say 200m until clear of the edge, then north again on the original bearing until clear of the edge feature on the map, then back east for 200m, which would bring one back onto the original line: three sides of a square.

A dog-leg is similar but is two sides of a triangle, achieved by selecting a point that will take one well out to the side of the cliff, then a second bearing and pacing to bring one back onto the original line, the other side of the hazard. It requires careful bearings and pacing in poor visibility. Marking a dot on the map with a permanent pen to help provide a target to measure distance and bearing to and to start the second leg, is a good idea. If visibility is fine, one would probably just follow the edge. With a small feature like a marsh one may be able to identify an obvious feature on the far side in line with the bearing, or a group member could go around it and be

Figure 4.3 Competitors in mountain marathon events use many navigation strategies

lined up by the leader on the bearing. The rest of the group then walk around and resume the bearing.

Five D's of navigation?

In addition to the strategies above, an overview of planning a leg can be supported by the Five Ds of route planning (although you may come across anything from three to seven of them). It seems to be most often used in the context of communicating a navigation leg in a succinct manner (probably to an assessor). However, there may be an argument that using this distracts people from thinking about their strategy: attack points, catching features and aiming off. Distance and direction measurements may lead to straight line thinking, compass in hand and counting paces. Good navigators follow the easiest going underfoot which will involve weaving around but generally maintaining a rough direction through looking well ahead to an obvious attack point.

- **Description** – What is the destination likely to look like, what should we see or feel?

- **Distance** – How far roughly – across grid squares or measure for accuracy?

- **Direction** – Estimate it – what is the bearing?

- **Duration** – How long will it take, timing or pacing?

- **Dangers** – Are there any hazards to be avoided?

Figure 4.4 Winter conditions call for well-honed skills

Summary

All of the above strategies are often used in combination, so the skill is in selecting the right combination to give one the best chance of finding the target yet keeping it simple and efficient.

To practise these, an orienteering map can be ideal as it will provide plenty of opportunities to use and experiment with these techniques. Navigating in woodland means that there is an element of realism as the target is often hidden until close by.

Study a local orienteering map and mark a circuit of short legs incorporating these strategies. Check it out first, then take the group for a map-and-compass walk round it, practising the skills.

Section 5: Relocation Skills

We all get 'temporarily geographically embarrassed' or 'cartographically challenged' at times but it is the ability to relocate ourselves that is important. When people walk with the map in their rucsac, one would presume that their relocation skills must be excellent because whenever they do take it out, they will need to employ a relocation technique. Unfortunately however, this seems to be the skill which is often the least understood and least practised, yet can be a life saver.

Figure 5.1 Navigating at night in the winter needs a full range of strategies and ability to relocate effectively

The principles of relocation
Maintaining contact with the map not only prevents getting lost in the first place, it also improves or maintains navigation skills. Quite often something obvious on the ground is not marked on the map, such as a small but obvious knoll. Maintaining contact with the map enables much more information to be collected so there is much less chance of being disorientated. Subtly one also learns to get an idea of the limitations of maps and the process of mapping. What appear to be anomalies are more easily reconciled.

There is always sound advice such as 'return to your last known point'. Fine, on a line feature, but sometimes this is not practical. It is simply too far. When really lost this is not an option.

Work out how long you have been travelling since your last known position. Knowing your speed-of-travel and rough direction could enable you to narrow down a possible location. For direction, can you recall the wind direction on the forecast? What has been your direction-of-travel in relation to it? Or where has the sun been, and where should it be in relation to where you were going?

Much of it is detective work, checking the map and the ground and eliminating possibilities. Quite often using a relocation skill such as slope aspect does not tell you where you are. Rather, it tells you where you are not and often indicates you are in one of a couple of different places. Then the detective work begins and may require walking further to gain more information to complete the puzzle.

You have to **move to prove** or **travel to unravel** your location.

A top tip is: **Spend 2/3rds of the time looking at the ground and only 1/3 of the time looking at the map.**

You can memorise a square km of a map in seconds but it often takes much longer to absorb 360 degrees of ground shape and features around you.

> **A progression of relocation skills**
> There are three stages:
>
> 1. Set the map (using the ground or compass)
>
> 2. If on a line feature, take a bearing along it
>
> 3. If in open ground/hillside use slope aspect
>
> If the first one does not begin to help, move on through the list. 2 and 3 can be used simply for confirmation of location or as the start of unraveling a totally lost situation.
>
> Ultimately for speed and efficiency the key is to select the most appropriate single method for the situation.
>
> Lastly, get lost and practise relocation skills so they are not a jumbled panic response! Do this in a relatively safe environment with an orienteering-type map, so the distances involved will be relatively short, and plenty of additional information is available. On the hill, a GPS with digital mapping can provide a back up to confirm if you have relocated accurately.

Resections or back bearings

Traditionally teaching resections was done in the classroom by taking bearings on obvious map features that supposedly one could see in the distance, and then drawing lines down the side of the compass to create a cocked-hat triangle to indicate your position. In reality, if visibility is good enough to see three prominent features, one is not really lost.

However, whilst sceptical of this relocation technique, it can be useful if standing on a line feature such as a stream, ridge or path (or even a contour line, if you have an altimeter). It is not particularly accurate, but drawing lines can be skipped as one line is already present, i.e. the linear feature. Take a sighting bearing on a visible known feature, ideally at right angles to the linear feature and turn the dial for a fine bearing. Place the compass on the map, keeping the base plate on the feature that was sighted on; move the base plate until the lines in the housing match the north grid lines and N to the top of the map. (The needle can be ignored unless you want to set the map). Where the compass baseplate crosses the linear feature is roughly where you are. These techniques have to be developed and practised **on the ground** using an organised, methodical and practised response to being 'lost'.

Teaching and developing relocation skills

The idea of relocating can start from drawing the map in the classroom when people change seats, or using the nine-cone exercises, or even on the map walk, all of which are mentioned in the first part of the book- all part of the confidence building process.

Once familiarity has been gained using the compass for bearings, then the techniques are very similar to that process. The methodology tends to be the reverse of the bearing process and both quick and accurate bearings can be used.

A quick bearing process: Point the baseplate along the line feature, e.g. a track, bring the map up under the compass, using the needle to set it. The map can be slid around under the compass. Watch to see which track aligns best with the compass edge. This may seem awkward to begin with for those who have done some navigation in the past. They are more used to moving the compass around on top of the map rather than moving the map around under the compass.

An accurate bearing: point the base plate along the line feature, e.g. a track, and turn the dial until Fred is in his shed. Place the compass on the map ensuring the lines in the capsule are aligned with the north–south grid lines (the needle does not need to be pointing to the top of the map, although that would indicate the map was set). Slide the compass around on the map looking to see which track lines up best with the edge of the compass keeping the capsule lines aligned with the north-south grid lines.

It may not be conclusive, so a plan is required to prove the conclusion, most probably to travel along it until a definite point can be identified such as a bend or junction.

The best way of developing relocation skills is to go on a map walk. Ask the group not to use their maps and proceed to get them increasingly disorientated, or let one of the group lead. Ideally use a wood you know well and lead them through the trees from track to track. At each track or line feature ask them to locate where they are. It is best done with a 1:10,000 scale map with plenty of alternatives, where the process can be repeated quickly lots of times. Later, the same thing can be done on the hill with a 1:50,000 map.

Once students have grasped the taking of bearings along line features and putting that back onto the map, they will quickly pick up the slope aspect technique, especially if the concept has been drip fed when contours were first introduced. Use a small hilltop where you can look down in a number of different directions in close proximity to the top. This way is usually possible to get at least four slope aspect exercises in quick succession.

Another slope aspect exercise is to pre-set a slope aspect on the compass and then walk, usually traversing around a slope, to match it to the ground. If you wanted to descend a hill in the mist and you were on the north side above difficult ground which could be avoided on an easterly aspect, pre-set an east bearing on your compass, from the map if necessary. Point the compass baseplate accurately down the slope. The red end of the needle will not be aligned to N on the dial but if you traverse around the hillside to the easterly aspect it will slowly come around to align to the N on the dial. You can then descend safely, crossing the contours at right angles. This is using slope aspect as a linear feature, a catching feature or an attack point.

Section 6: Orienteering - an overview

Figure 6.1 Orienteering is a good way to develop navigation skills, and have fun!

I doubt if this book would have been written without the recent development, proliferation and availability of orienteering maps. They are the game-changing tool for teaching navigation and breaking away from traditional map reading skills based on the needs of the military. Many educational establishments and urban parks now have their grounds mapped, and even some villages and small towns have been mapped by local club members. There are also over 500 Permanent Orienteering Courses (POCs) around the UK with most POC maps being downloadable free from the British Orienteering website.

British Orienteering has a range of orienteering formats from the traditional orienteering forest events to Xplorer events for youngsters, Park orienteering and Sprint orienteering, and Trail Orienteering for all abilities. Within those, apart from the traditional linear type events, there are also relays, night events and score events (where everyone starts together, planning their own route, aiming to visit as many controls as possible in a set time).

There are round 130 Clubs around the UK largely based on county boundaries. There are local regional and national events, many are open to anyone, and events like the Scottish 6 days will attract in excess of 3,500 competitors from age 9 to 90!

Although this is a club-based sport, anyone can go along to a local club competition, pay the entry fee which includes a map to keep and, these days, renting an 'SI card'. This is a tiny electronic device that fits on your finger and records your visit to each control. At the end it is downloaded and produces a print out of the controls you visited and the time you took

between each one. This encourages people to review their strategies, compare their times and route choice and is a great source of learning. Something hillwalkers tend not to do.

There is no requirement for club membership or evidence of competence. Club competitions usually listed as category D or C events are very much family-friendly events and organisers are always keen to help newcomers. Walking around a course as a pair practising the skills, wearing outdoor walking clothing, is completely acceptable and commonplace. Most clubs nowadays run a weekly or monthly evening training session, where club coaches help members improve their technical navigation skills.

At local events one usually just pays for the map on arrival. Often these are annotated as EOD 'entry on day'. Regional ones often require a pre-entry online but usually accommodate people turning up on the day as well.

The sport is carefully coached so that the skills step system which has 5 TD (Technical Difficulty) levels is mirrored by a colour coded choice of courses. At the upper end there is 5+, but this is more a case of increasing the course length. There are parameters that guide the course planner in designing the routes which also have to be independently checked on the map and on the ground. The notion is that if the guidelines are followed, a Green course in Sussex should feel the same as a Green course in the Highlands of Scotland.

The Orienteering TD1 to 4 in the rough table (Figure 6.2) are not that different from the table on page 4 in this book. TD1 and TD2 are largely map skills, keeping to linear features and ticking off features, measuring distances using a compass for setting the map. TD3 the compass is used for short distances introducing quick bearings, attack points, catching features and aiming off etc.

For families there is a 'string' course for little children with an adult: about 500m following tapes around easy paths. Very occasionally there is a 'red' option which is a long yellow/orange for runners and a 'black' which is longer than 'brown'.

For anyone going through Mountain Training awards, as a rough guide, the TD level for an ML training candidate should be Light Green, and Green is ML assessment level.

Light Green is a really good starting point for adult

newcomers who have navigation competence. It provides good route choices, to follow linear features or go cross-country with compass skills and strategies.

Beware of looking at the distances quoted, and quickly deciding that 5+ km would be good value-for-money, and estimating being around an hour. These distances are measured as a direct line between controls. Contours are not taken into account although height gain is calculated and quoted. Even without being misplaced, it is likely that you will be stood still at each control for at least a minute planning the next leg (although you should have been doing a bit of that during the last leg, but at least move away from the control so as not to advertise its location to others). Lastly, running just tends to mean mistakes are bigger before you realise them, but it is good for practising those relocation skills in a safe and reasonably confined area!

The table in Figure 6.2 is helpful to give an understanding of how navigation skills development links to the complexity of a leg that a tutor might set their students. It also provides a degree of safety management and confidence for the tutor so that participants can be challenged at the right level.

Benchmarking navigation legs against the distance from an attack point and catching features is an interesting element of the orienteering system and not replicated in other recreational schemes involving navigation. We will never find a whole series of the perfect legs but a benchmark provides a standard which recognises a difficult or easy leg. It creates general criteria to work to and transparency for the planner or tutor and the student.

Technical Difficulty	Colour Code	Distance	Guidance for course difficulty
TD1	White	1- 1.9km	Controls on easy line features, at regular intervals and at every decision making point.
TD2	Yellow	2- 2.9km	Controls on line features and at most but not all decision making points.
TD3	Orange	2.5- 3.5km	Controls are off line features but should be within a 50m bracket of an attack point and catching feature behind it. An option to cut corners between line features and obvious contour features can be used.
TD4	Light Green	3- 4km	The 50m bracket moves to 100m. There is route choice between long distance on line features or shorter cross country options between controls and more contour interpretation and strategies needed.
TD5	Green	3.5- 5km	The 100m bracket moves out to around 200m either side of the control and route choices will mostly be cross country and all skills are required including complex contour interpretation.
TD5+	Blue	5.5- 7.5km	Longer legs with complex route choice.
TD5+	Brown	8- 12km	As for Blue with more of everything!

Figure 6.2 A rough guide to Orienteering courses linked to the Technical Difficulty

Section 7: Teaching Resources

Map walk using an orienteering map

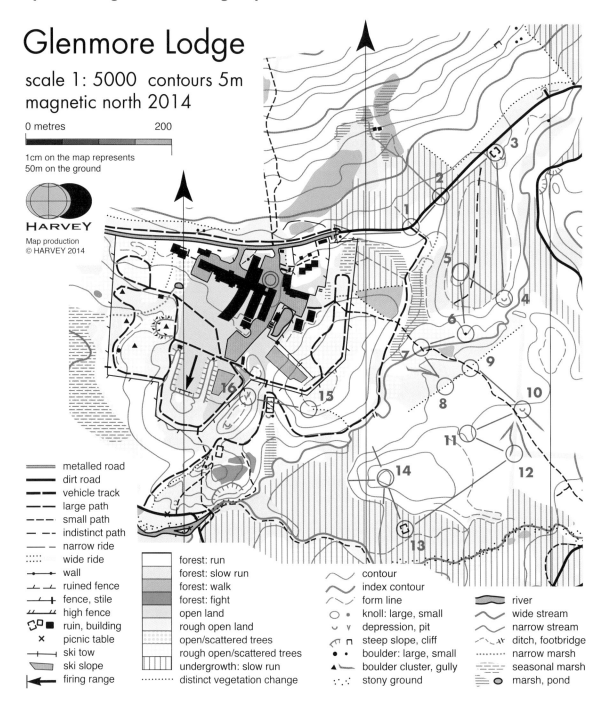

Glenmore Lodge

scale 1: 5000 contours 5m
magnetic north 2014

0 metres   200

1cm on the map represents
50m on the ground

HARVEY
Map production
© HARVEY 2014

metalled road	
dirt road	
vehicle track	
large path	
small path	
indistinct path	
narrow ride	
wide ride	
wall	
ruined fence	
fence, stile	
high fence	
ruin, building	
× picnic table	
ski tow	
ski slope	
firing range	

forest: run	
forest: slow run	
forest: walk	
forest: fight	
open land	
rough open land	
open/scattered trees	
rough open/scattered trees	
undergrowth: slow run	
distinct vegetation change	

contour	
index contour	
form line	
knoll: large, small	
depression, pit	
steep slope, cliff	
boulder: large, small	
boulder cluster, gully	
stony ground	

river	
wide stream	
narrow stream	
ditch, footbridge	
narrow marsh	
seasonal marsh	
marsh, pond	

Figure 7.1 Maximising an orienteering map

16 navigation legs in less than 2km: a map walk developing strategies and skills. The tutor can set the different legs, letting students practice different skills at each leg, or students could take turn to lead. Students can use a blank or marked map. Walking maps would give 2 -4 legs for the route depending on the scale.

1. Prove pacing for 100m.

2. Pacing odd distances 65m.

3. Catching feature ridge contour interpretation.

4. Route choice, hand rail stream, change in contour steepness, attack point off knoll (5), quick bearing, catching feature.

5. Quick bearing.

6. Aiming off, contour interpretation.

7, 8, 9 & 10. Practice simple relocation skills - check direction of hand rail features.

11. Quick bearing and pacing, contour interpretation.

12. Aiming off for ride junction.

13. Ticking off features collected by stream aiming off.

Up to 14. Slope aspect x 3.

Across to 15 with maps away, relocate starting with slope aspect.

16. Route choice: attack point and catching feature.

Home.

Useful equipment

The Classroom and Basic equipment
- Ideally a simple room with a number of tables and a chair per person
- Computer /projector for PowerPoint presentation (Provide at venue)
- A1 flip chart, paper and pens (Provide at venue)
- NNAS Tutor Handbook
- Paper and pens/pencils
- Permanent marker pens, cloth and small bottle of white spirit/meths for cleaning laminated cards (not if flying)
- Blu-Tack
- Elastic bands and small bulldog clips for keeping card sets together
- A range of compasses
- Maps of local area, ideally orienteering maps

Introduction
- Ice-breaker – laminated chopped-up maps of several scales, laminated map legends
- Control markers for a classroom – small plastic or laminated squares (available from Harvey Maps)

Map Setting
- N. (S. E. W) Large laminated signs for classroom walls. A5 or A4
- 12 cones or equivalent (nine required)
- Clothes pegs or grips (just a couple, for example to help monitor card/map setting, if required)
- Nine-cone laminated cards 12 pairs (available from Harvey Maps)
- Orienteering maps of the local area or street map

Contours
- Surgical glove for introducing contours
- Laminated contour cards for sand/plasticine modelling
- Scissors and white string
- Hill model: stacked tiles and A1 sheet with contours drawn and N. S. E. W.
- 2 x 30m white ropes or clothes lines
- Contour-only maps, for example only
- British Orienteering contours handout sheets

Compass Work
- Classroom bearing sheets for compass bearings (tend to use paper for folding and retention by attendee)
- Nine-cone laminated cards for bearings
- Directional laminated cards for three different compass exercises
- A few bin bags for Walking on a Bearing exercise
- Compass course cards, and golf tees

Other Resources
- A few laminated sets of map memory cards
- A range of maps
- A range of navigation and orienteering teaching books

Books, teaching resources and equipment

Books

Outdoor Navigation Handbook for Tutors
Pat and Brian Mee
ISBN 978-185137002-3

Teaching Orienteering
Carol McNeill, Jane Corey-Wright, Tom Renfrew
ISBN 978-0-88011-804-0

Navigation in the Mountains
Carlo Forte
ISBN 978-0-9541511-5-7

Look at the Harvey Maps and British Orienteering websites for other books around the teaching of navigation.

Websites

www.nnas.org.uk
National Navigation Award Scheme – Bronze Silver and Gold. The Bronze is now on the SQCF at Level 4 worth 2 credits.

The NNAS tutor hand book, Outdoor Navigation, is the best teaching navigation book commercially available.

Teaching resources, compasses, maps

www.harveymaps.co.uk
Maps, books e.g. NNAS Tutor Handbook, teaching resources, teaching games, classroom control markers, nine-cone waterproof card sets, contour only maps, navigation aids

www.compasspoint-online.co.uk
Online shop – quality compasses, spare base plates, pacing clickers, magnifiers etc.

www.ordnancesurvey.co.uk
Information on maps, teaching navigation, access etc.

www.citylab.com/design/2016/06/con-tour-lines-hutton-schiehallion/486308/
An explanation of the origins of contour lines

Organisations

www.britishorienteering.org.uk
Events information – your local club England and Wales, Schools Orienteering, and resources.

Teaching orienteering part 1 (TOP 1) and part two (TOP 2) and UKCC coaching awards. Coaching resources

www.scottish-orienteering.org
Scottish Orienteering Association (SOA) events, clubs etc.

www.bsoa.org
British Schools Orienteering Association

www.bmbo.org.uk
British Mountain Bike Orienteering Association

www.theaward.org/scotland
Duke of Edinburgh's Award scheme

www.glenmorelodge.org.uk
Scotland's National Outdoor Training Centre, located in Cairngorms National Park.

www.mountain-training.org
For all mountain award trainees and holders – Mountain Training Association (MTA) advice and CPD opportunities.

www.rgs.org
Royal Geographical Society – Geography today section

www.catchingfeatures.com
Download the demo and have some fun

Mapping software to help create maps

Some of these may help to create a base map so further detail can be added by hand.

www.streetmap.co.uk

digimap.edina.ac.uk
Digimap is a collection of EDINA services that deliver maps and map data of Great Britain to UK tertiary education.

This is a great resource enabling the creation of an orienteering type map of the school.

www.oomap.co.uk
Orienteering mapping software

www.purplepen.golde.org
Orienteering mapping software

www.ocad.com
Orienteering mapping software

www.openorienteering.org
Free orienteering mapping software

www.openstreetmap.org
Mapping software

Google Earth is also a useful tool for map making and interpretation.

NOTE Most mapping is copyrighted and copying other than for personal use may require a licence.

Online resources for teaching contours

www.scottish-orienteering.org/natcen/page/infor-mation-and-resources-for-coaches
Visit the coaching resources in the Scottish Orienteering website. There are some classroom exercises in there.

www.rgs.org/webcasts/activities/contours/con-tours.html
An interactive quiz.

www.ordnancesurvey.co.uk/mapzone/map-skills/relief-and-contours/page-six
There are a number of resources on the Ordnance Survey website.

YouTube has a lot of orienteering and teaching navigation clips, some more helpful than others. Search for "sand box terrain contours".